SEVENSTEPS
TO BE MADE WHOLE

Dr. Craig M. Morgan

HighWay

A division of Anomalos Publishing House

Crane

HighWay
A division of Anomalos Publishing House, Crane 65633
Printed in the United States of America
08 1
ISBN-10: 0981495729 (paper)
EAN-13: 9780981495729 (paper)

Cover illustration and design by Steve Warner

A CIP catalog record for this book is available from the Library of Congress.

DEDICATION

I dedicate this book to our Heavenly Father, the Lord God Jehovah, who is the one true Living God. I thank Him for choosing me to be His tool to write this and for giving me this message. My prayer is that I have been able to express what He wants without tainting it in any way. May it be received as such by all who read this. Indeed, all glory and honor to our Lord forever and ever, and ever.

Contents

FOREWORD

The wholeness God intended for us to experience in our lives was lost to sin in the beginning—in the Garden of Eden. Due to God's original plan and because of the brokenness left behind by sin, we have a natural proclivity to desire wholeness again. Innate in each of us is an instinctive longing to be complete. We all want to put the pieces back together and operate at a level that will bring meaning to our lives.

Searching for wholeness can be a futile, lifelong endeavor if we take the wrong path, arriving at one empty finish line after another. We look to others to make us whole through our various relationships. We search for wholeness in our careers or in making more money. To aid in our quest to discover wholeness, we even pour ourselves into books in an effort to achieve the highest educational level. We do all of these things and many others because inside we know that we are meant to be whole. We also know that if we ever do become whole, we will attain a level of satisfaction that will bring us the fulfillment, which nothing prior has been able to accomplish.

However, all we really need is the correct path, one that will compel us to focus on God and search His Word for the answers we crave. Since He is the one who has created us with the desire—this voracious appetite for wholeness—He is the only hope of fully satisfying that inherent longing. All of us have gone astray, but as we submit to Him, the empty places are filled and our destiny restored.

Dr. Craig Morgan has given us great insight in this area through his thorough study and vast knowledge of the Word of God. His straightforward, well-educated approach leaves no stones unturned as he takes you through biblical illustrations and practical examples that will leave you excited about what God really has in store for you. He leads you past the brokenness you have experienced in your lifetime and toward the fullness God has destined for you.

In this powerful book, Dr. Morgan provides not only an accurate compass, but also a step-by-step process based on truths found in the Word of God, which will lead you to self-study and reflective prayer in your pursuit of the wholeness that God has designed for all of us. Dr. Morgan presents these truths in a way that you will not only grasp, but also internalize. The revelation you experience will give you the power to walk out these steps on the right path to a rewarding and fulfilling life, that gives glory to God as well.

—Chuck Lawrence

ACKNOWLEDGMENTS

would like to acknowledge those who have been important to me in my development as a Christian and in my walk with God. Besides giving us Himself, the greatest way that the Lord blesses us is by our family and the people He brings into our lives. There have been many who have truly blessed me. I would like to thank my parents, who raised me in a Godly manner and introduced me to our Lord, and my wife and family who have not only allowed me to spend time with God, but have encouraged me to do so. Obedience to God costs those around us more than it does ourselves. I thank the spiritual mentors that the Lord has placed in my life. They opened my eyes to know that there was more to be had with God than what I knew, and my heart to hunger for Him. I thank you, Mildred Battle and Linda Blevins. I thank my spiritual prayer and fellowship with God partners with whom we have shared much in the Lord: Melissa Goodrich, Mack Gillenwater, Aimee Chapman, and Pastor Kevin West among many. And of course, my pastor, Chuck Lawrence. He is much more than a pastor; he is my spiritual mentor. I rest under his authority, but I am also privileged to call him my friend. I thank Karen Salters who has allowed me to share with her much of what the Lord has given me and was responsible for typing this manuscript. To all these, and the many others who have touched my life, I say thank you, and may the Lord bless and truly reward you for what you have done!

INTRODUCTION

Often when Jesus healed people, He would simply tell them that they were healed or that their faith had healed them. At other times, however, as with the woman experiencing the issue of blood, He told them that they were whole. They were not just healed, but made whole.

What then is the difference between being healed and made whole, and what does it mean to be whole?

As James wrote, to be whole means that you are "…perfect and entire, lacking nothing" (James 1:3–4, King James Version). If you are whole you do not need to be healed, because you have health. If you are whole you are an overcomer and as such, you are entitled to all the rewards Jesus reveals to us in the book of Revelation, chapters 2 and 3. To be whole means that you have achieved rest in God, walking in and enjoying the promises that He has given us. It means to have victory in our lives now and authority over our adversary, the devil (satan). It means to be absolutely perfect in the eyes of God!

In this book, Craig Morgan will show you the seven steps to achieving wholeness as revealed to him by the Lord. These seven steps are chronological in order and are based on the patriarchs of the Bible. They are (1) to walk with God as Enoch; (2) to be a friend of God as Abraham; (3) to become a prayer as Joseph; (4) to become a man of God as Moses; (5) to have the heart of God as David; (6) to have the love of God as John; and (7) to know God as Paul. These steps are ones that all believers must take if they are to progress in their walk with, and knowledge of, God in all that He desires us to do and have. The Lord will illuminate you on your journey to know Him, and to be whole for this is His desire for all of us.

In the writing of this book, Craig has chosen not to capitalize the name or any reference to satan because satan does not warrant that, or any other type of honor or respect.

chapter one

TO BE MADE WHOLE

...wilt thou be made whole?

— J O H N 5 : 6 , K J V

Healing was an important part of Jesus' earthly ministry. The Scripture states repeatedly that He healed all that came to Him. On occasion when Jesus healed someone, He would say that they were healed as with the Centurion's servant. We read in Matthew 8:13, "And Jesus said unto the Centurion, Go thy way; and as thou hast believed so be it done unto thee. And the servant was *healed* in the self same hour" (emphasis added).

However, at other times when Jesus healed someone, He did not just heal them, but rather made them whole. For example, this is given to us when Jesus healed the woman with the issue of blood. Jesus did not just heal her; he made her whole. Matthew 9:22 reads, "But Jesus turned him about, and when he saw her, he said, 'Daughter be of good comfort; thy faith hath made thee whole.' And the woman was made whole from that hour."

Nothing is in the Bible by accident. Therefore, there must be a difference between being healed and made whole. What then does it mean to be made whole?

The Greek word for whole is *sozo*. Sozo is defined in *The Strong's Concordance* as "to save, i.e., deliver or protect (literally or figuratively);—heal, preserve, save (self), do well, be (make) whole." Therefore, sozo is also used to refer to the salvation of souls. It means to save, heal and make everything whole. Literally, it means to enable a person to become a totally whole person!

Sozo is used to refer to deliverance from danger, suffering and sickness. It refers to God's power to deliver from the bondage of sin. It also refers to all the blessings God has given us through Christ.

To be whole then, is to be in health so that one does not have to seek healing. To be whole means that one is "…perfect and entire, wanting nothing" (James 1:4, KJV). To be whole is to be an overcomer (Revelation, chapters 2 and 3, KJV). When one is whole they have obtained a walk with, and entered into the rest of, God. When one is whole they have allowed the cross to work in their life. They have lost self-consciousness and obtained Christ consciousness. Indeed, when one is whole they have all the blessings God has given us through Jesus.

The apostle Paul knew this when he wrote I Thessalonians 5:23, which reads, "And the very God of peace sanctify you wholly; and I pray God your whole spirit and soul and body be preserved blameless unto the coming of our Lord Jesus Christ."

Here the Greek word for wholly and whole, as used in the verse, is *woloteles*. Woloteles in *The Strong's Concordance* means "complete to the end, i.e. absolutely perfect." To be whole is to be absolutely perfect in the eyes of God!

Who then would not want to be whole? All who are serious in their walk with God do. However, our Lord would ask us the same question now that He asked the man at the pool of Bethesda. In John 5:6, we read that Jesus asked him, "...wilt thou be made whole?" The answer would seem obvious, easy and certain. However, it must not be so obvious and easy or Jesus would not have asked that question.

There are, in fact, seven steps that each of us must take to become whole in the eyes of God. These seven steps are based in chronological order on some of the great patriarchs in the Bible. They must be taken in sequential order. In other words, one cannot progress to step two until one has completed step one and so forth. For each step more is required, but the reward is far greater as well. Ultimately, what is required is the completion of the cross in our lives and the death to ourselves. Many are not willing to take this road, though the rewards are great if we do.

Herein are the words that the Lord has given me to share with you. They are meant to exhort and edify us on our journey with Him. These are the seven steps to be made whole.

These seven steps are: (1) To walk with God as Enoch; (2) to become a friend of God like Abraham; (3) to become a prayer like Joseph; (4) to be a man of God as Moses; (5) to have the heart of God as David; (6) to know God and His love as John; and finally (7) to know God as Paul.

Wholeness is a product of the Holy Spirit, but it cannot come until our own desire sets it in motion. "Wherefore, my beloved, as ye have always obeyed, not as in my presence only, but much more in my absence, work out your own salvation with fear and trembling. For it is God which worketh in you both to will and to do of his good pleasure" (Phil. 2:12–13, KJV). Let us begin to explore together these seven steps so that we, too, may become whole and achieve all that God wants us to be!

ARE YOU READY TO BE MADE WHOLE?

There was a man of the Pharisees, named Nicodemus, a ruler of the Jews: The same came to Jesus by night, and said unto him, "Rabbi, we know that thou art a teacher come from God: for no man can do these miracles that thou doest, except God be with him." Jesus answered and said unto him, "Verily, verily, I say unto thee, Except a man be born again, he cannot see the kingdom of God." Nicodemus saith unto him, "How can a man be born when he is old? Can he enter the second time into his mother's womb, and be born?" Jesus answered, "Verily, verily, I say unto thee, Except a man be born of water and of the Spirit, he cannot enter into the kingdom of God."

—JOHN 3:1–5, KJV

Before one can become whole, one must enter the Kingdom of God. To do so, one must be redeemed by the Blood of the Lamb, the Lord Jesus Christ. One must become born again or saved. If you are not, I invite you to do so now. It will be the best decision you have ever made and one that you will never regret.

SALVATION MESSAGE

Do you know Jesus? Do you know Jesus as your personal Lord and Savior? If you were to die tonight, do you know if you would be going to Heaven or not? If you cannot say for sure that you know that you will be going to Heaven, if you do not know Jesus as your personal Lord and Savior, my hope and prayer for you is that you do so now.

God's way is a way of simplicity. There is but one way toward salvation. There is but one way to spend eternity in Heaven, and this is to accept Jesus as our personal Lord and Savior. This is the only way. Simple? Yes. The only way? Absolutely! We cannot enter into Heaven by being good. We cannot enter into Heaven by works. We cannot work at it. The only way is to be redeemed by the Blood of Jesus. God is a God of justice and judgment. He demands restitution for sin as the wages of sin are death. However, first and foremost, God is a God of love. God provided us with a way so that we can be redeemed and that our sins may be forgiven. It required a sacrifice, and God sent His Son Jesus to be this sacrifice for us. John 3:16 reads, "For God so loved the world, that he gave his only begotten Son, that whosoever believeth in him should not perish, but have everlasting life."

We are all sinners. The purpose of the law was to show mankind that we are sinners and that we could not save ourselves. Only Jesus can save us. The steps for salvation and eternal life in Heaven are simple. We must first realize that we are sinners and have fallen short. We then must repent of our sins and express sorrow for them. We must desire to have our sin removed from us and to change so that we sin no more. We then must believe in Jesus. We must believe that Jesus was God, the Son of God, and He was made human and born as a miraculous virgin birth by his mother, Mary. Jesus, the Son of God, became a son of man, so that we, the sons of men, could become the sons of God. Jesus came to teach and show us the way. We must believe that Jesus was crucified, dead and buried. The Blood that He shed for us on the cross is what covers our sin. We then must believe that Jesus rose from the dead and that He ascended to Heaven where He sits at the right side of the Father. Jesus died for us on the cross so that our sins may be forgiven, and He rose into Heaven so that we would know that we could also rise if we just believe in Him.

I pray that the Holy Spirit has convicted you and given you the faith to accept this truth. The simple truth is that we will all spend eternity in one place, either Heaven or hell. God, through His love for us, wants us to spend eternity with Him in Heaven. He loves us so much that He sent His Son to die for us in order that we could be saved and go to Heaven with Him. Please accept this simple truth. None of us are guaranteed tomorrow. None of us know if we will wake up tomorrow morning or not. Tomorrow may be too late. Please accept this truth now. If you are ready, just pray a simple prayer to God. Ask Him to save you. You may pray in the following manner:

Oh God, I know that I am a sinner. Please forgive me of my sins. I do not want to continue with my old life. I want a new life in you. I believe that Jesus was my substitute when He died on the cross. I believe that His shed blood, death, burial and resurrection were for me. I now receive Him as my Lord and Savior. I thank you for the forgiveness of my sins, the gift of salvation, and everlasting life. Amen!

God's power will save and enable you to live a victorious Christian life. Do not trust your feelings, for they change. Stand on God's promises, for they never change.

After you are saved, there are three things to practice daily for spiritual growth:

1) Pray. You talk to God and He talks to you.
2) Read your Bible. God reveals Himself to you in the Bible. You learn of His ways. You learn His will, and you learn of His person.
3) Witness. You talk for God.

You should be baptized in obedience to the Lord Jesus Christ as a public testimony of your salvation. Then unite with a Bible-believing church where the presence of God is without delay.

I pray that your life has been forever changed. Mine was!

As we journey through these seven steps to become whole, our fervent commitment to the Lord will increase. Before we begin this journey, if you are not serving our Lord as you know you should be, now is a good time to rededicate yourself to Him.

REDEDICATION MESSAGE

Do you believe that you are right with the Lord? Are you walking with God? Have you reached the Promised Land that God wants for you? Are you walking in the promises of God that He has given you? Do you desire more of God? Do you desire a deeper relationship with Him? If so, I invite you to rededicate yourself to Him.

It is God's desire for us to have an intimate relationship with Him. It is His desire that we be one with Him, that we know Him, and that we fulfill His will for us. I certainly have not arrived where I need to be in my walk with God, but He has given me a hunger for Him that cannot be satisfied with anything else. I understand what David meant when he said, "One thing have I desired of the LORD, that I will seek after; that I may dwell in the house of the LORD all the days of my life, to behold the beauty of the LORD (to see Him face to face and be with Him mouth to mouth), and to inquire in his temple (to get to know Him)" (Ps. 37:4, KJV).

Have you felt the presence of God? Have you been in His presence? If so, then you will know what the psalmist meant when he said one day in the presence of the Lord is greater than a thousand days elsewhere (Ps. 84:10, KJV). Simon helped to carry Jesus' cross (Luke 23:26, KJV). It is recorded in the book of Josephus that he was asked what it was like to have carried the cross, for it must have been a heavy load. It is estimated that the cross weighed between 300 and 400 pounds. Simon answered, "While I was carrying the cross He touched me. Jesus touched me. I would carry that cross a thousand times just to feel His touch once again" (Ps. 37:4, KJV). This is how I feel. This is what the Lord wants for each of us. Saints, it is possible. It is God's desire. It can be our desire, and we have His word that He will give us the desires of our heart if we delight in Him.

God has awesome plans for us, and His plans are to only make everything better for us. His plans are to bless us abundantly above and beyond what we can even dream. He has given us a will however, and He rarely will contradict that will. It is His will that it be our will to seek Him.

If you are not where you want or need to be in your walk with the Lord, I would ask you to search yourself and commit to Jesus today. The Word declares in Isaiah that we are to call upon the Lord while He is near, and seek Him while He may be found (Isa. 55:6, KJV). Call upon Him now. Consecrate yourself to Him. When you consecrate yourself to Him, you give the Holy Spirit permission to work in you and to fill and change you. Give yourself to Jesus. Give yourself totally to Jesus. Ask Him to change you. It is a decision that you will never regret. Every aspect of your life will be better. Examine yourself and dedicate yourself to Jesus. Invite Him and give Him permission to enter into a deeper relationship with you. We are instructed to abide in Him, and if we do, He will abide in us. We are to be the branch of Him, the

Vine. The Vine supplies everything essential to the branch that is necessary for the branch's existence. This is what God will do for us if we abide in Him.

Judges 16:22 reads, "Howbeit the hair of his head began to grow again after he was shaven." Charles Spurgeon eloquently discusses this verse as follows:

> Many a man I have seen come back to the dear Savior on account of the oppression which he has endured from his old master, the prince of darkness! If he had been treated well, he might never have returned to Christ anymore; but it is not possible for the citizens of the far country to treat prodigals well; sooner or later they starve them and oppress them, so that they run away home. When Samson's hair began to grow, what did it prophesize? Well, first, it prophesized hope for Samson. I will be bound to say that he put his hand to his head, and he felt that it was getting bristly, and then he put his hand to his beard, and found it rough. Yes, it was coming, and he thought within himself, "It will be alright soon. I shall not get my eyes back. They will not grow again. I am an awful loser by my sin, but I shall get my strength back again, for my hair is growing. I shall be able to strike a blow for my people and for my God yet." So round the mill he went, grinding away, grinding away, but every now and then putting his hand to his head, and thinking, "My hair is growing; Oh, it is growing again! My strength is returning to me."

The mill went round merrily to the tune of hope, for he felt that he would get his old strength back again. Then they loaded it, and tightened it to make the work heavier, yet his hair was growing; and so he found the burden lighter than it had been before, and his heart began to dance within him, in prospect of being his former self again. Now, if any of you have signs of restoring grace in your hearts, and you are coming back to your God and Savior, be glad. Be thankful. Do not hesitate to let your renewed devotion to God be seen by those around about you. If the grace of God is moving you at all, be hopeful and quicken your steps, and come to Jesus. Come to Him just now even as you came at first. (Used with permission from Kregel Publications, all rights reserved: Al Bryant, *Day by Day with C. H. Spurgeon* [Grand Rapids, MI: Kregel Publications, 1992], 35–36.)

Saints, God is calling you now. Please answer Him. Living your life for Jesus is a decision that you will never, never regret.

chapter three

STEP ONE:
TO WALK WITH GOD AS ENOCH

He hath shewed thee, O man, what is good; and what doth the
LORD require of thee, but to do justly, and to love mercy,
and to walk humbly with thy God?

—MIC. 6:8, KJV

Micah tells us in Micah 6:8 what the Lord requires of a believer. This verse reads, "He hath shewed thee, O man, what is good; and what doth the LORD require of thee, but to do justly, and to love mercy, and to walk humbly with thy God?" Here the Lord commands us "…to walk humbly" with Him.

The Bible says that two men did, in fact, walk with God. These two were Enoch and Noah. In Genesis 5:22 we read that Enoch walked with God. "And Enoch walked with God after he begat Methuselah three hundred years, and begat sons and daughters", and in Genesis 6:9 how Noah walked with God as well: "These are the generations of Noah: Noah was a just man and perfect in his generations, and Noah walked with God."

Enoch though, was special. Not only did Enoch walk with

God, but he became so close in his walk with God that he was translated to Heaven. This is given to us in Genesis 5:24 which reads, "And Enoch walked with God: and he was not; for God took him."

In Hebrews 11:5, it is recorded how Enoch was translated. He was living by faith in God. "By faith Enoch was translated that he should not see death; and was not found, because God had translated him: for before his translation he had this testimony, that he pleased God." Enoch became so close to God, walking with Him, that he pleased God. As a result, he did not die. Rather, God took him directly to Heaven.

As we will see, faith is the key in everything with our relationship with God. The next verse in Hebrew reads, "But without faith it is impossible to please him: for he that cometh to God must believe that he is, and that he is a rewarder of them that diligently seek him" (Heb. 11:6, KJV).

Since Enoch walked with God, He could use him as He willed. Enoch was a prophet. He saw Jesus return before Jesus even came. This is given to us in Jude 1:14–15, which reads, "And Enoch also, the seventh from Adam, prophesied of these, saying, 'Behold, the Lord cometh with ten thousands of his saints, To execute judgment upon all, and to convince all that are ungodly among them of all their ungodly deeds which they have ungodly committed, and of all their hard speeches which ungodly sinners have spoken against him.'"

Before we progress further, let us stop and indeed consider Enoch and his relationship with God. As Enoch matured in the natural, he also matured spiritually in his relationship with God. God called him forth and Enoch answered. Enoch separated himself from his family and others, and would walk with God. There they walked with one another. They fellowshipped and communed with each other. Gradually, their walks and time together became longer. Each, both God and Enoch, began to look forward to their walks together, and their time together grew more and more important. I can only begin to imagine what the Lord shared with Enoch and how Enoch, excited as a child opening presents on Christmas morning, received what God revealed to him. Enoch could not wait to go back and walk with God again.

Eventually, their time became so precious to each of them that they did not want to part. In fact, they could not part. Therefore, God extended an invitation to Enoch. He asked Enoch to leave the world behind, forsaking the blessings of the world that He had given him, and come home with Him now. God did not want to be without Enoch, and Enoch did not want to be without God. I do not believe that Enoch hesitated. I believe that he accepted our Lord's invitation immediately. God said, "I need you with me now Enoch, constantly."

And Enoch said, "I do too, Lord."

So God extended His hand and Enoch reciprocated. He reached and grabbed God's hand, and God took him to Heaven. He was translated. He did not die the death that is appointed to all men, because he walked with God. He became so close with God that God took him home so they could be with each other continually.

Let us ponder on the significance of this. This moment moves me to tears. Enoch, a man just like us, became so close to God by walking with Him that God could not do without him. Likewise, Enoch could not exist without God, and the Lord took him home.

This is what God wants when He commanded us to walk with Him. We should desire, as Enoch did, to have this personal relationship with our Lord and indeed walk with Him.

What does it mean exactly to walk with God? At the beginning, it means to fellowship with Him. It means to commune with Him. It means to share all that you have with Him. It also means that you listen and allow Him to share Himself with you.

In All the Prayers in the Bible, Herbert Lockyer comments on this as follows:

With God as his traveling companion Enoch must have maintained unbroken communion with God. The same is also true of Noah, who like Enoch walked with God. In Genesis, chapters 6–9, God is found doing all of the talking and no reply from Noah is recorded. The repeated statement about Enoch walking with God suggests that he was a progressive saint. For walking implies progress, spiritual progress, that is dependant upon unbroken communion with Heaven. The Hebrew word for walking signifies "to go on habitually". This progress and holiness was the habit of this ancient saint. Amid the cares of family life and the corruptness of their time, both Enoch and Noah pleased God.

To begin with, to walk with God we must like Him enough to do so. He is the Holy One. If we want to walk with Him, we must allow Him to work with us enough to break us, to have the fullness of the cross worked in us, and to advance to the resurrection phase of our spiritual life.

Amos 3:3 reads, "Can two walk together, except they be agreed?" Indeed, this is true. You cannot walk with someone in companionship unless you are in agreement with them. This means that you have to know someone to be in agreement with them. You have to be in like mind and accord. This places a responsibility on us as well, to be able to walk with God. God is holy indeed, and to be able to walk with Him, to be in agreement with Him, we have to be made holy by Him ourselves.

Before the fall, Adam and Eve walked with God. They were naked in the natural, but did not know it. They were sinless and did not know what sin was. Indeed, they were created in God's image and likeness. Therefore, they had a glorified body as our Lord Himself has. They were clothed with God's righteousness and holiness. They were clothed with God's presence and glory.

In the cool of the day, Adam and Eve walked with God in the garden. There, God revealed Himself to Adam. There, he taught Adam. There, their relationship was nurtured and developed. There, Adam acquired so much knowledge that he was able to name every living creature of the earth. This is an insurmountable task. Most of us struggle with naming our pet. There are millions of creatures on the earth, and Adam named them all. He acquired this knowledge by walking with God and allowing God to impart

Himself, and His very nature, to Adam. Therefore, in order for us to walk with God, we have to have God's characteristics imparted into us through Jesus as well. After the fall, Adam lost this relationship with God. He no longer walked with Him.

Moses tells us in Deuteronomy, chapter 13, that there are six steps in our relationship with God. These six steps in sequential order are to: (1) fear God; (2) obey God; (3) love God; (4) serve God; (5) walk after God; and (6) cleave unto God (Deut. 13:4, KJV). We must always remember these steps in order to walk with God successfully. We must not forget them, especially our fear of the Lord. This is a healthy fear. This is not a fear that He will harm us. We are not afraid of God. Rather, it is a respect of God and His magnitude and authority. We must never underestimate God or take Him for granted.

King Asa did just this. Many feel that it is impossible to be perfect, and that only our Lord Jesus was. However, in the Bible we are commanded to be perfect (Deut. 18:13, KJV). God has never given us a command without giving us the ability to fulfill it. The same is with being perfect. Four men are mentioned as being perfect in the Bible. They are Noah (Gen. 6:9, KJV); David (I Kings 15:3, KJV); Job (Job 1:1, 1:8 and 2:3, KJV); and King Asa (I Kings 15:14, KJV).

In II Chronicles, chapter 16, we read of King Asa. He became sick. Specifically in II Chronicles 16:12, we read that his feet were diseased. This was in the natural realm, of course. However, what happened and preceded this was that King Asa stopped walking with God in the spiritual realm. Since he stopped walking with God in the spiritual realm, eventually he came to the point where he could no longer physically walk with Him in the natural realm. Indeed, his feet were diseased! Instead of seeking God, he sought his physicians. As a result, King Asa died.

King Asa forgot to maintain a proper relationship with God. He was called perfect by God. He walked with God once, but when he lost his fear of God, when he lost his relationship with God, when he lost his fellowship and companionship with God, then he stopped walking with God. He returned to the world and stopped seeking God. As a result, he died.

There is but one way to walk with God and that is by faith. This is given to us in II Corinthians 5:7, which reads, "For we walk by faith, not by sight." Indeed how simple, but eloquent. We walk not by sight, but by faith. This is our key to walking with God. To walk with God, we must walk as Jesus did. Many Christians want to continue in their old lives. To walk with God, one must abandon all this. If we are to have the presence of God, we must walk as Jesus walked. If this is our heart's desire, Jesus will walk with us. As long as we want to walk on a lower level than Jesus, as long as we want to have a little of this world and a little of self rule, we cannot expect to have the presence of Jesus with us, nor can we walk with God. Praise be to God, though. Jesus invites us to come and have this unbroken fellowship with Him in order that we may walk with God.

In II Samuel, chapter 5, we read where David captured Jerusalem from the Jebushites. After doing so, David declared that "...The blind and the lame shall not come into the house" (II

Sam. 5:8, KJV). "…The house" was the house of God. We see the requirements to be able to come into the house of God. First, we must see. The blindness David referred to here was spiritual blindness. Therefore, we must be saved or born again before we can begin our progress with God. However, the lame could not come into the house of God either. We must walk with God in both the spiritual and natural realms before we can come into His presence.

David knew this when he wrote Psalms 25. In verses 4–5 we read, "Shew me thy ways, O Lord; teach me thy paths. Lead me in thy truth, and teach me: for thou art the God of my salvation; on thee do I wait all the day." This is walking with God. To truly walk with God, we must grow in our life so that we are prostrate before Him in both the soul and spirit. Walking with, hearing and following God are forms of worship. Walking with God makes us sons of God. This is what others are looking for. Indeed, the steps of a righteous man are ordered by God. "The steps of a good man are ordered by the LORD: and he delighteth in his way" (Ps. 37:23, KJV).

In Revelation, chapters 2 and 3, the Lord gave seven letters to the seven churches. These were literal letters to seven churches which existed at that time. However, these were also for the church for all time, and for us as individuals as well. In Revelation 3:4 we read, "Thou hast a few names even in Sardis which have not defiled their garments; and they shall walk with me in life: for they are worthy." There are a few which have, are, and will walk with God. They will forsake the world. They will seek their Lord and they will walk with God. To those that do, God will call them worthy. For those that do, He will clothe them in white signifying purity and holiness (Rev. 3:5, KJV).

Remember that Enoch was over 350 years of age when he was translated. Although it does not take that long for us, it does take time and a commitment on our part to walk with God. It is a gradual step-by-step process and will not happen overnight.

As Oswald Chambers wrote in *My Utmost for His Highest*: "In learning to walk with God, there is always the difficulty of getting into his stride, but once we have done so…the individual person is merged into a personal oneness with God, and God's stride and His power alone are exhibited."

To walk with God as Enoch did should be the aspiration of us all. Reflect once again on the magnitude of Enoch's relationship with God. They were companions, yet much more. By faith, Enoch was translated from one world to another. So too, are we by faith. When we walk with God, we can be translated from the natural world to the spiritual world. We now can be translated from the natural world into God's very presence and throne room by faith. Our high calling is not in our service for God. Rather, it is knowing God. Enoch discovered this. He lived it!

Indeed, let us walk with God as Enoch did!

chapter four

STEP TWO:
TO BE A FRIEND OF GOD AS ABRAHAM

And the scripture was fulfilled which saith,
Abraham believed God, and it was imputed
unto him for righteousness:
and he was called the Friend of God.

—JAMES 2:23, KJV

fter you walk with God, you can then become a friend of God like Abraham was. In James 2:23 we read, "And the scripture was fulfilled which saith, Abraham believed God, and it was imputed unto him for righteousness: and he was called the Friend of God." Additionally, II Corinthians 20:7 states the same. This verse reads, "Art not thou our God, who didst drive out the inhabitants of this land before thy people Israel, and gavest it to the seed of Abraham thy friend forever?"

What does it mean to be a friend of God? In John 3:29 we read, "He that hath the bride is the bridegroom: but the friend of the bridegroom, which standeth and heareth him, rejoiceth greatly because of the bridegroom's voice: this my joy therefore is fulfilled." This, of course, refers to Jesus, and the bride is the church. But to the friend of the bridegroom, to the friend of Jesus, is given a special position and the Master's joy.

In John 15:13–15 we read, "Greater love hath no man than this, that a man lay down his life for his friends. Ye are my friends, if ye do whatsoever I command you. Henceforth I call you not servants; for the servant knoweth not what the Lord doeth: but I have called you friend; for all things that I have heard of my father I have made known unto you." What wonderful things are outlined in these verses! First, in verse 13 our Lord states that there is no greater love that a man can exhibit than to lay down his life for his friends. It is very unlikely that in the natural we will be called to do this. However, all of us must do this for our friend Jesus. We must forsake all, die to self, and lay down our life for Him. Continuing in verse 14, Jesus tells us how to become His friend. It is simple. Obedience. He simply states, "You are My friend if you obey and do whatever I command you."

What is the reward for first laying down our life and sacrificing all for our friend Jesus, and secondly for unconditionally obeying Him so that we may become His friend? The reward is that He calls us friend. We are no longer His servant, but His friend. And as His friend, He will reveal to us what the Father has revealed to Him. Without being His friend, you cannot have revelation knowledge.

Additionally, as we read previously in James 2:23, Abraham became a friend of God because of his faith in God. Due to his faith in God, he was then willingly obedient. He left all to go to the Promised Land, which he never found. Yet, he walked by faith through obedience. Due to his faith and obedience, the Word of God declares that it was imputed unto him righteousness. He was therefore called a friend of God.

What being a friend of God means is given to us in Genesis, chapter 18. In verse one we read, "And the Lord appeared unto him in the plains of Mamre: and he sat in the tent door in the heat of the day." Here the him in this verse is Abraham. The Lord appeared to Abraham "…in the plains of Mamre…" Continuing in verses 2–3 we read, "And he lift up his eyes and looked, and, lo, three men stood by him: and when he saw them, he ran to meet them from the tent door, and bowed himself toward the ground, And said, 'My Lord, if now I have found favour in thy sight, pass not away, I pray thee, from thy servant.'" This reinforces what we have discussed previously. If you are a friend of God, He will reveal Himself to you. Additionally, He will appear to you. He will make Himself known to you. Not only that, but God will bring His angels with Him or command His angels to meet your needs. He will provide for you just as any friend would help and provide for their fellow friend.

In these verses we see that Abraham recognized the Lord equally. As soon as Abraham looked up and saw the three men, he knew that one of them was the Lord who was Jesus. No introduction was necessary. At this point, he had already known God. He knew Jesus. He had already encountered Jesus. He knew who Jesus was, so as soon as he saw Jesus, he immediately ran to Him, bowed down and called Him "my Lord". He already knew Jesus intimately. He had fulfilled step one. He had walked with God.

He had walked with Jesus. He had seen Him face to face. He recognized Him, immediately knew who He was, and ran to Him.

Continuing in Genesis 18:4–5 we read, "Let a little water, I pray you, be fetched, and wash your feet, and rest yourself under the tree, And I will fetch a morsel of bread, and comfort ye your hearts; and after that ye shall pass on: for therefore are ye come to your servant. And they said, 'So do, as thou hast said'" (Comfort: Hebrew stay). A relationship with a friend is reciprocal. Your friend will help you, but you want to help your friend as well. So it is with the Lord. Only few realize that we can bless the Lord. Here, Abraham in the physical was tending to and serving the Lord. He was blessing the Lord. He washed the Lord's feet. He prepared a place for Him to rest and fed Him. Specifically, the Word of God declares he comforted God. There are times when the Lord has a heavy heart. During these times, He will come to us if we have a relationship with Him. If we are friends with Him, then we can comfort Him. We can serve and bless Him.

In Genesis 18:16 we read, "And the men rose up from thence, and looked toward Sodom: and Abraham went with him to bring them on the way." Abraham was walking with the Lord and His angels. Again, the first step to being made whole is to walk with God. If you are a friend of God, you are welcome to walk with Him, which is what the Lord wants us to do.

Continuing in Genesis 18:17–18 we read, "And the Lord said, 'Shall I hide from Abraham that thing which I do; Seeing that Abraham shall surely become a great and mighty nation, and all the nations of the earth shall be blessed in him?'" What magnificent verses. If you are a friend of God, He will not hide from you. If we are friends with God, we will be able to find Him, and we will allow Him to find us. There, God will share intimate things with us that He will not with others. He will not hide things from us, for we read in Amos 3:7 "Surely the Lord GOD will do nothing, but he revealeth his secret unto his servants the prophets." God will reveal His secrets to us, His servants, if we are a friend and walk with Him.

Continuing in Genesis 18:19, we see why the Lord felt that Abraham was a friend, could be trusted, and why God felt He could reveal things to Abraham. This verse reads, "For I know him, that he will command his children and his household after him, and they shall keep the way of the LORD, to do justice and judgment; that the LORD may bring upon Abraham that which he hath spoken of him." When you are a friend of God, you will obey Him. You will fulfill His will, and you will do it without questioning Him. If a true friend of yours needs and asks for help, you will give it to him. A true friend of God will obey God, do what He asks and fulfill His will. The Lord knew that Abraham would do this. This verse states that He knew Abraham would command his children and household after him to keep the way of the Lord, and to do justice and judgment.

If we are submissive in spirit and obedient in flesh, and are a friend of God, then the Lord can bring upon us that which He has spoken of for us, just as it states in verse 19 that He would bring upon Abraham that which He had spoken of and for him. A prophecy does not mean that it will absolutely be fulfilled. It means that something should and may be fulfilled, but it is not necessarily fulfilled. The Bible is replete with instances where the Lord gave prophesies to someone. Yet, because they were not friends of God, and they did not walk with God, these prophecies were not fulfilled. Due to disobedience, they were not a friend of God. As a result, that which God had spoken to them, the promises of the Lord for them, were not fulfilled. This was true in the case of Nebat's son, Jeroboam, who was Solomon's superintendent over taxes. Jeroboam was promised by God that if he would walk with and obey the Lord, and do what was just and right, then he would be as strong and powerful as Solomon. This was a promise from God and potential for Jeroboam. However, Jeroboam did not do this. He went to the ways of the world. He did not walk with God. He was not a friend of God. Therefore, this promise of God, this prophesy from God, was never fulfilled in Jeroboam's life.

In verse 19 we read that the Lord would bring upon Abraham that which he had spoken to him. When you are a friend of God, the promises of God will be fulfilled in your life. If you are not a friend of God, and you are disobedient, then they will not be fulfilled. The initial promise was given to Abraham's father. Abraham's father did not fulfill the commandments that God had asked him to do, however. Therefore, the promise was not given to Abraham's father. Instead, it was given to Abraham, because Abraham walked with and was a friend of God.

In Genesis 18:20–33 we read of the Lord's wrath toward Sodom and Gomorrah. We also read in these verses that Abraham was the intercessor for their citizens. The Lord said that He was going to destroy Sodom and Gomorrah. In verse 23, Abraham asked the Lord if He would destroy the righteous with the wicked ("And Abraham drew near, and said, 'Wilt thou also destroy the righteous with the wicked?'"). Continuing, he asked the Lord that if he could find fifty righteous people, would God spare these fifty that were there, and the Lord said "yes" (Gen. 18:24–26, KJV). When Abraham realized that there were not 50 righteous people, he asked the Lord if the Lord would spare 45 righteous people, and the Lord said "yes" (Gen. 17:27–28, KJV). Then Abraham realized that there were not 45 righteous men, so he asked the Lord if He would spare 40, and the Lord said "yes" (Gen. 18:29, KJV). When Abraham saw that he could not find 40, he asked the Lord if He would spare 30. Next it was 20, and finally it was 10 (Gen. 18:30–32, KJV). After agreeing to spare the city if Abraham could find 10 righteous men, the Lord went His way (Gen. 18:33, KJV).

Intercession is the greatest gift and opportunity that the Lord has given us. We have the Lord's assurance now, as in the book of Hebrews, that Jesus is sitting at the right hand of God the Father, and is interceding for us daily. The Lord has given us the opportunity to intercede for others. However, we have to be a friend of God before we can effectively intercede for others. This is also given to us in the parable of the importunate friend as recorded in Luke 11:5–14. Here we read in verse 5, "And he said unto them, 'Which of you shall have a friend, and shall go unto him at midnight, and say unto him, Friend, lend me three loaves.'" Here we see the two friends. The second friend, the one capitalized, is Jesus. The other is our friend in the natural. We can go to our one true friend, the one who will never abandon, forsake or leave us, Jesus, and petition Him for our other friends. This is when we truly intercede.

Returning to Genesis 18:27 we read, "And Abraham answered and said, 'Behold now, I have taken upon me to speak unto the Lord, which am but dust and ashes.'" Although we are a friend of God, we must realize our proper place. Abraham knew this. In this verse Abraham was saying, "I am nothing but dust and ashes. I realize that Father. I realize that you are Lord God almighty, but allow me the privilege as your friend to come to you and intercede on the behalf of others."

In Genesis 18:33 we read, "And the Lord went his way, as soon as he had left communion with Abraham: and Abraham returned unto his place." This is the relationship the Lord wants to have with us that was stolen from man with Adam's original fall. He wants to commune with us. When you are a friend of God, you can commune with the Lord. Here the Lord went His way as soon as He finished communing with Abraham, and Abraham returned to his own place.

Friendship is rare on earth. It means similar identity, thought, heart and spirit. The entire discipline of life is to enable us to enter into this close relationship with Jesus Christ. We may receive His blessings and know His Word, but do we know Him? When we obtain intimacy and friendship with Jesus, we are never lonely. We never need sympathy. We can always minister to others.

You cannot become a friend of anyone without knowing that person intimately and tangibly. That is why Abraham was visited by Jesus. It was also so that Jesus could know him tangibly as well. The Lord will visit each of us if we are serious in becoming His friend. *providentially bless*

If we are a friend of God, we will be in contact with Him so that we will never need to ask Him to show us His will. We can then decide things in perfect delightful friendship with God, knowing that if our decisions are wrong, He will always tell us. When He does, we should obey Him immediately.

In the RSV Translation of the Bible, Psalms 25:14 reads as follows: "The friendship of the LORD is for those who fear him, and he makes known to them his covenant." God offers intimate and lasting friendship to those who reverence and hold Him in highest honor. What relationship could ever compare with having the Lord for a friend? However, a lasting friendship with God will grow as we reverence Him.

To be a friend is a covenant partner. To be a friend, we must have faith. This is where Abraham learned faith. In fact, Abraham is called the father of faith.

Romans 5:10 reads, "For if, when we were enemies, we were reconciled to God by the death of his Son, much more, being reconciled, we will be saved by his life." The NLT Translation of this verse reads as follows: "Since we were restored to friendship with God by the death of his son while we were still his enemies, we will certainly be delivered from eternal punishment by his life."

As Rick Warren in *The Purpose Driven Life* writes, "God wants to be your best friend. Your relationship to God has many different aspects: God is your Creator and Maker, Lord and Master, Judge, Redeemer, Father, Savior and much more. But the most shocking truth is this: Almighty God yearns to be your friend!"

Friendship with God is possible only because of the grace of God and the sacrifice of Jesus.

Rick Warren continues and states that there are six secrets of being a friend with God. These are: (1) through constant conversation with God; (2) through continual meditation on and about God; (3) to be honest with God; (4) to obey God in faith; (5) to value what God values; and (6) desire friendship with God more than anything else (*The Purpose Driven Life*, 85–99).

Proverbs 17:17 reads, "A friend loveth at all times, and a brother is born for adversity." Concerning this verse, Frances Roberts writes,

Endurance is native to those who love, for to truly love is to continue to love under all circumstances. Man's natural love is often an exchange, a mutual giving and receiving; but God's true holy love will give when there is no exchange because it does not require reward and is not motivated by gifts. Love gives because it is its nature to give and so is not a respecter of person or conditions. "A friend loveth at all times" and because he does, he endures. He endures hardship, pain, privation, poverty, weariness, misunderstanding and sacrifice of personal wishes and needs...He continues to give and continues to love giving, and in so doing he is preserved in the day of adversity. He is preserved from doubts, fears and questionings. He is protected against discouragement. He is strengthened in weakness and sustained in trouble. He is invincible and loves in the sustaining force. He endures, for he who sees Him who is invisible…Him who is the epitome of love, is at one with the Creator and receives continuing creative power which is the secret of his endurance. To be one with the source is to have an unfailing supply. (*Make Haste My Beloved*, 23)

To be a friend of God…It does not seem possible that a mere mortal man could be a friend of the omnipotent, omniscient and omnipresent One. Yet, this is His desire for us. It should be our desire as well. It requires faith and total obedience. It requires unconditional love, but the rewards are great. He will call us friends. We may call Him friend, and there we can intercede for Him and others.

James 4:4 reads, "You adulterous people, don't you know that friendship with the world is hatred toward God? Anyone who chooses to be a friend of the world becomes an enemy of God." Here we are told clearly that to become a friend of God, we must separate and set ourselves apart from the world and for God. There is a cost to be paid to be God's friend.

Joyce Meyer writes:

It is obvious some people are closer to God than others. These close friends of God speak of talking to Him as if they know Him personally. Their faces shine with enthusiasm as they testify, "And God told me . . ." while skeptical acquaintances grumble to themselves, "Well, God doesn't talk to me like that!" Why is that? Does God have favorites? No, scripture teaches that each person determines his or her own level of intimacy with God, depending on their willingness to seek Him and put time into developing a relationship with Him. Everyone has been extended the same invitation to "Let us therefore come boldly to the throne of grace, that we may obtain mercy, and find grace to help in time of need" (Heb. 4:13, KJV). At this moment, you are as close to God as you choose to be.

Likewise, Rick Warren writes: "Like any friendship, you must work at developing your friendship with God. It won't happen by accident. It takes desire, time, and energy. If you want a deeper, more intimate connection with God you must learn to honestly show your feelings with Him, trust Him when He asks you to do something, learn to care about what He cares about, and desire His friendship more than anything else." (*The Purpose Driven Life*, 85–99)

Remember, "Draw nigh to God, and he will draw nigh to you . . ." (James 4:8, KJV).

Indeed, as Joyce Meyer and Rick Warren have written, we determine our level of intimacy with God. Specifically, it is determined by how we seek Him. Several times in the Scripture it states that we will find God when we seek Him with our whole heart. I have found this to be so true. Unequivocally, I feel the presence of God more when I seek Him the most. And it does not always have to be a lengthy seeking either. He recognizes our schedules. There are times when we cannot go to the prayer closet for an extended period of time. We can, however, always seek Him fervently and passionately, even if but for a short period of time.

Let us all aspire to be a friend of God as Abraham was!

chapter five

STEP THREE:
TO BECOME A PRAYER AS JOSEPH

Praying always with all prayer and
supplication in the Spirit, and watching thereunto
with all perseverance and supplication for all saints.

—EPH. 6:18, KJV

After we have become a friend of God, then we can move on to the next step. Not only can we move on to the next step, but we must. The next step is to become a prayer like Joseph.

We will not confuse this with being The Prayer. Jesus Himself is The Prayer. It is possible, however, to become a prayer.

There is no record in the Word of God of Joseph ever having said a prayer. However, no one could have endured the temptations, tests, trials and tribulations which Joseph did, and overcome them the way he did, without being in prayer. I believe that the only way he could have achieved the success that he did and have the faith that he had during these tests, trials, temptations and tribulations, was that he was in constant prayer. That is why there is no record in the Bible of an uttered prayer spoken by him to God. He had, in fact, become a prayer. Jesus is The Prayer.

Joseph, however, had become a prayer. God calls and woos us to become a prayer as well.

The apostle Paul directed us to do this. As you will see, Paul himself had become a prayer. That is why he wrote for us in Ephesians 6:18, the following command: "Praying always with all prayer and supplication in the Spirit, and watching thereunto with all perseverance and supplication for all saints."

As a result of Joseph becoming a prayer, we see that Joseph was able to name his two sons as he did. He named his first born, Manasseh. This is given to us in Genesis 41:51. This verse reads, "And Joseph called the name of the firstborn Manasseh: For God, said he, hath made me forget all my toil, and all my father's house" (Manasseh: that is, Forgetting). He named his second son, Ephraim. We read of this in Genesis 41:52, which reads, "And the name of the second called he Ephraim: For God hath caused me to be fruitful in the land of my affliction" (Ephraim: that is, Fruitful).

What awesome blessings God gave Joseph. Certainly, Joseph went through much more anguish than many, if not most, of anyone who has ever lived. He was sold by his brothers, enslaved, falsely accused and imprisoned. Yet, because of his relationship with God, because he walked with God, was a friend of God and had become a prayer, God blessed him and enabled him to forget all of his trouble and toils. God didn't stop there, however. "…For God also hath caused me to be fruitful in the land of my affliction." Not only did God give him the grace to forget his afflictions and furthermore forgive those that had harmed him, but God caused him to prosper and be fruitful in the enemy's camp. Luke clarifies this even further for us in Acts 7:9–10. These verses read, "And the patriarchs, moved with envy, sold Joseph into Egypt: but God was with him, And delivered him out of all his afflictions, and gave him favour and wisdom in the sight of Pharaoh, King of Egypt; and he made him governor over Egypt and all his house."

If we will trust in God and lean not to our own understanding, if we will become one with Him through constant prayer, if we pray unceasingly as we are commanded to do, then this will happen to us as well. The only way to do this is to become a prayer. If we become a prayer as Joseph did, then we can do what he did and have the same things that he had. God can send us into the heart of the enemy's camp and protect us. Not only can He send us into the enemy's camp and protect us from any harm, but He will allow us to prosper there as well.

Joseph was comforted so much by the Lord through all of his severe trials, tests and tribulations that he was able to call his firstborn son Manasseh, for the Lord had indeed caused him to forget all of his troubles. Furthermore, he named his second son Ephraim, for the Lord had caused him to prosper in the face of the enemy. The land of the enemy was where his affliction occurred, but he prospered even there, because God is faithful. God will do what He started and said He would.

As exciting as this is, there is still more. In Genesis 41:55 we read, "And when all the land of Egypt was famished, the people cried to Pharaoh for bread: and Pharaoh said unto all the

Egyptians, 'Go unto Joseph; what he saith to you, do.'" This command should sound familiar. In the second chapter of the gospel of John, we see the record of the first miracle that Jesus performed where at the wedding feast He changed water into wine. Verse five is a verse that we should all commit to memory. This verse reads, "His mother saith unto the servants, 'Whatsoever he saith unto you, do it.'" We know that God requires obedience. He will settle for nothing less. Indeed, when He tells us to do something, whatever it is, we should not think, but just immediately do it.

Jesus is the Lord God Almighty and the King of the Saints (Rev. 15:3, KJV). He is the Lord of Lords and the King of Kings (Rev. 17:14, KJV). In John 2:5, Jesus' mother told the servants that whatsoever Jesus said to do, do it. The servants were therefore told that whatever the King said to do, do it. Mary, Jesus' mother, told the servants that whatever the King said to do, they should immediately do it.

Returning to Joseph, the Pharaoh, or King of the Egyptians, told the Egyptians or servants that whatever Joseph said to do, they should do it. This exact same phrase is used in both places. Mary told the servants that whatever the King said to do, do it. The King of the Egyptians told the servants that whatever Joseph said to do, they were to do.

Saints, this is possible for us. If we become one with God, if we become a prayer warrior in communion with Him and have established a relationship of walking with Him and being His friend, then we are so one with Him, that the King will tell the servants, whatever we say to do, do it. God will know that one who is in communion with Him, that one who is a prayer with constant prayer to Him, will speak what God wants him to speak. The Prayer, Jesus, through constant communion by us becoming a prayer, will speak to and through us so that we can become His mouthpiece. We will speak what the Father says. Then the King will tell the servants whatever we say, do it.

This is possible. It is possible not only to aspire to have, but to achieve this level of intimacy with God. It is possible to be His mouthpiece. It is possible to be in communion with Him. It is possible to pray unceasingly, or He would not have commanded us to do so. It is possible to become a prayer.

To become a prayer like Joseph means that we live in full harmony with God. God put men like Joseph in the Bible for us to know that it is humanly possible for us to achieve the same that they did. God is no respecter of persons (Acts 10:34, Rom. 2:11 and Eph. 6:9, KJV). If He did it for Joseph, He can and will do it for us. He asks us to have a seeking heart. He asks us to have no idols before Him. He will honor those that honor Him (I Sam. 2:30, KJV). Yes, it is possible. We should aspire to achieve the unlikely in God. That is His desire. Joseph did it, and so can we. Then we can be God's mouthpiece. Then God, the King, will tell the servants, whatever we say, do it. "As for me, this is my covenant with them, saith the LORD; my spirit that is upon thee, and my words which I have put in thy mouth, shall not depart out of thy mouth, nor out of the mouth of thy seed, nor out of the mouth of thy seed's seed, saith the LORD, from henceforth and for ever" (Isa. 59:21, KJV).

Jesus again is The Prayer. The disciples got a glimpse of Jesus as the divine intercessor and The Prayer. When they saw Him pray, they realized that He lived for prayer. In fact, prayer was the air that Jesus breathed. He inhaled the presence of God. He exhaled exaltation, intercession, admonition and encouragement to the Father in Heaven. His whole life flow was prayer. Just as the fullness for all things dwell in Jesus, a true fullness and prayer dwells in Him also.

Jesus gave His life to prayer. Likewise, we as His followers can be certain that it is His desire to bring each of us into the same passion for prayer. We tend to think of prayer as something that we need to do to meet our demands and needs. To Jesus, prayer was His need. Prayer was His agenda. Nothing touched Him like communion with His Father. He wanted His disciples, us, to follow His lead.

Frances Roberts writes the following: "The life which you draw from God is like the sap in the tree which must be drawn from the bosom of the earth. Sever the roots from the source, and death ensues. Even so, the spiritual dependency of your soul upon Him, though unseen, is every bit as real. Draw upon Him. It is His desire to sustain you. It is His will and His design. It is your only hope, your only comfort. It is PRAYER!"

"And he shall be like a tree planted by the rivers of water, that bringeth forth his fruit in his season; his leaf shall also not wither; and whatsoever he doeth shall prosper" (Ps. 1:3, KJV).

Joseph became a prayer. As such, the King told his servants that whatever Joseph said to do, they were to do. Since he was a prayer, the Lord delivered him from his times of affliction and caused him to prosper, even in the middle of the enemy's camp. The call is for us to become a prayer today as well. If we will answer God's call and go forth and achieve it, then God will give us the same blessings that He gave Joseph. Let us indeed become a prayer!

STEP FOUR:
TO BE A MAN OF GOD LIKE MOSES

And this is the blessing, wherewith Moses
the man of God blessed the children
of Israel before his death.

—DEUT. 33:1, KJV

After becoming a prayer, one must progress on. The next step is to become a man of God, like Moses.

Moses yielded incredible power as a man of God. He led the Israelites out of their bondage in Egypt. He accomplished this only as a man of God. He killed one Egyptian on his own. Yet, when he became a man of God, he delivered the entire nation of Israel as the vessel through which God worked.

Moses, because he had gone through the first three steps, was also a friend of God. The Word of God declares that Abraham and Moses were friends of God. Exodus 33:11 reads, "And the LORD spake unto Moses face to face, as a man speaketh unto his friend..."

As a friend of God, Moses could pray to God and intercede

for others. In fact, his greatest role was as an intercessor for the nation of Israel.

Two of the most profound prayers recorded in the Bible were prayed by Moses. The first is the ultimate prayer of intercession, which Paul also prayed.

This is given to us in Exodus, chapter 32. In this chapter, we read that while Moses was on the mount face to face with God, since he was a man of God, the Israelites in the camp under the direction of Moses' brother Aaron, made a golden calf and began to worship it. Not only that, but they turned it into a riotous drunken event. The Lord was aware of this and told Moses to go down from the mountain and deal with the people. "And the Lord said unto Moses, 'Go, get thee down; for thy people, which thou broughtest out of the land of Egypt, hath corrupted themselves'" (Exod. 32:7, KJV).

God then said, "They have turned aside quickly out of the way which I commanded them: they have made them a molten calf, and have worshipped it, and have sacrificed thereunto, and said, 'These be thy gods, O Israel, which have brought thee up out of the land of Egypt.' And the Lord said unto Moses, 'I have seen this people, and, behold, it is a stiffnecked people: Now therefore let me alone, that my wrath may wax hot against them, that I may consume them: and I will make of thee a great nation'" (Exod. 32:8–10, KJV).

What was Moses' response? What would be our response if we were in the same situation? Since Moses was more than a friend of God, but a man of God as well, he prayed to God. We read of this in the next verses as follows: "And Moses besought the LORD his God, and said, 'LORD, why doth thy wrath wax hot against thy people, which thou hast brought forth out of the land of Egypt with great power, and with a mighty hand?' Wherefore should the Egyptians speak, and say, 'For mischief did he bring them out, to slay them in the mountains, and to consume them from the face of the earth? Turn from thy fierce wrath, and repent of this evil against thy people. Remember Abraham, Isaac, and Israel, thy servants, to whom thou swarest by thine own self, and saidst unto them, I will multiply your seed as the stars of heaven, and all this land that I have spoken of will I give unto your seed, and they shall inherit it for ever'" (Exod. 32:11–13, KJV).

Moses knew that his people had done wrong. He could have acquiesced to the Lord's demand. Instead, as the ultimate intercessor, he petitioned God on their behalf.

What was the Lord's answer? If you ask people if the Lord has ever repented universally, everyone will say no. The Lord is infallible. He makes no mistakes. There is no need for Him to repent. Yet, three times the Word of God declares that God did repent, twice in the book of Amos and once here.

What was the Lord's response? "And the Lord repented of the evil which he thought to do unto his people" (Exod. 32:14, KJV).

With his prayer, Moses saved the entire nation of Israel. One man, because he was a man of God, had this much power in his petition of God. Due to this one man's prayer, the entire nation of Israel was spared.

Did God need to repent? No. But, God has set forth a principle that He can do nothing until His hands are moved by prayer. He knew that Moses would petition Him in this way, and Moses did. This shows us unequivocally the power that prayer has.

In James 5:16 we read, "Confess your faults one to another, and pray one for another, that ye may be healed. The effectual fervent prayer of a righteous man availeth much." Who is a righteous man? A righteous man is one who is a man of God. The prayer that Moses prayed was certainly an effectual fervent prayer. He was a righteous man, and indeed his prayer did avail much.

There are many other examples of the power of Moses' prayers. When Miriam and Aaron came against Moses, the Lord judged them sternly and strickened Miriam with leprosy. What was Moses' response? He could have gloated, as most of us would have been inclined to do. Instead, he cried out passionately to God. "And Moses cried unto the Lord, saying, 'Heal her now, O God, I beseech thee'" (Num. 12:13, KJV). Certainly this was a fervent prayer. He fervently emphasized his petition by saying, "…I beseech thee." Once again, God answered his prayer.

Returning again to Exodus, chapter 32, Moses did descend from the mountain where he had been with God for forty days, and put an end to the blasphemous revelry that had occurred. What did he do next? He went back and petitioned God for his people. He, the ultimate intercessor, as a man of God. In Exodus 32:30–31 we read, "And it came to pass on the morrow, that Moses said unto the people, 'Ye have sinned a great sin: and now I will go up into the LORD; peradventure I shall make an atonement for your sin.' And Moses returned unto the LORD, and said, 'Oh, this people have sinned a great sin, and have made them gods of gold.'"

Yet, Moses did not stop there. The next words that Moses prayed to God are some of the most startling and revealing words in the Bible. In Exodus 32:32 we read, "Yet now, if thou wilt forgive their sin—; and if not, blot me, I pray thee, out of thy book which thou hast written." Here, what Moses said was, "Lord, I ask you to forgive their sins. Yet, I know, because I am a man of God, that not only are you a God of love but a God of justice. Therefore, if you cannot forgive their sin, then I ask you, Lord, that you substitute me for them. If you cannot forgive them, Lord, take my name out of the Book of Life and put their names in. Lord, I am willing to go to hell for eternity for them if that is what it takes to forgive them. I will sacrifice myself and being with You in Heaven for eternity, and instead will go to hell for eternity for my people."

What an incredible prayer. What an incredible gesture. What love! These were people that had given Moses great trouble. They were not easy people to deal with. Yet, because he was a man of God, he could pray this prayer. It is my prayer that I someday may be able to pray this prayer as well, especially for those that I do not know (it would have been impossible for Moses to have known all of the two million people that he brought out of Israel) and for those who have done evil things to me. I can say this prayer now for very few are precious to me, such as my immediate family. But, Moses said it for the entire nation of Israel.

However, this was one prayer that the Lord could not grant. In Exodus 32:33 we read, "And the LORD said unto Moses, 'Whosoever hath sinned against me, him will I blot out of my book.'" The fact that God told Moses no, does not reduce the magnitude of this heartfelt prayer in any way.

We know that Moses was close to God just because he could pray these prayers. He dared to ask God to repent, and God did. He dared to ask God to remove his name from the Book of Life if that is what it took to save his people. I wish that I were this close to God.

How did Moses become a man of God? For one, he was meek. In Numbers 12:3 we read, "Now the man Moses was very meek, above all the men which were upon the face of the earth." Meekness is in the spirit realm and is what obedience is in the flesh. Much is written about the meek and how important it is to God. One who is meek will be blessed by God. In Psalms 22:26 we read, "The meek shall eat and be satisfied: they shall praise the LORD that seek him: your heart shall live for ever," and in Psalms 25:9 it states, "The meek will he guide in judgment: and the meek will he teach his way." That should be the heartfelt cry for all of us. For the Lord to show us His way is promised to the meek.

Continuing in Psalms 37:11 we read, "But the meek shall inherit the earth; and shall delight themselves in the abundance of peace." Jesus said the same in the Sermon on the Mount when He said, "Blessed are the meek: for they shall inherit the earth" (Matt. 5:5, KJV).

Our Lord was meek Himself. In Matthew 11:29 Jesus stated, "Take my yoke upon you, and learn of me; for I am meek and lowly in heart: and ye shall find rest unto your souls." Therefore, one must be meek, submissive in spirit, and obedient in the flesh before one can be a man of God.

Continuing, Moses knew God. In Exodus 33:11 we read, "And the LORD spake unto Moses face to face, as a man speaketh unto his friend..." Moses knew God face to face. Few have, or do now.

This verse refers to an incredible intimacy Moses shared with God. It speaks of insights and revelations the Lord gave to Moses because of their bond. Moses spent entire days in God's presence seeking to know Him. According to David Wilkerson, "This tells us Moses 'saw' God (or knew Him) as no human had before. Moses was gaining an intimate knowledge and understanding of God's heart, because of the quality time he spent with Him." (*Where Do I Stand With the Lord?* World Challenge Inc. Publications, October 13, 2003.) Knowing God is a two-way street. He wants us to know Him, but He also wants to know us. He does, of course. He knows every word that we will speak before we say it. He knows us better than we know ourselves. But, as with a friend, it is a two-way street. Moses had this relationship with God. In Exodus 33:17 we read, "And the LORD said unto Moses, 'I will do this thing also that thou hast spoken: for thou hast found grace in my sight, and I know thee by name.'"

Moses developed this relationship with God because he wanted to know God more than he wanted to know anything else. In Exodus 33:13 we read, "Now therefore, I pray thee, if I found grace in thy sight, show me now thy way, that I may know thee, that I may find grace in thy sight: consider that this nation is thy people."

What was Moses' heart set on? It was that he may know God, truly and intimately.

Moses had the most to give up when he left Egypt. He was brought up by Pharaoh's daughter. He had all the amenities that the world had to offer. He was in line to serve as royalty. Yet, he gave it all up willingly to save and deliver his people and serve God.

On the other hand, the Israelites had nothing to hold them back in Egypt. They were slaves who were treated terribly. The Israelites, however, always clamored to return from the desert to Egypt. To them, the way of Egypt was better than the way of God.

Moses, who had the most to gain by going back to Egypt, never desired to do so. His desire was the desire of God. The Israelites were content with the promises that God had to make. They were content to eat from the hand of God. Moses was not. He wanted more. He insisted on more. He was not just satisfied with the promises or the hand of God. Rather, he wanted to know God face to face and heart to heart. "...Shew me now thy way, that I may know thee..."

Moses knew that God was faithful. Men of God do. Men of God do not fear natural enemies, but fear God with a righteous holy fear. After their exodus, God had Moses lead the people to the Red Sea. There they were camped. Pharaoh directed his troops to go after them to kill and destroy them, and recover the treasures that the Israelites had taken from Egypt when they left. The Israelites were in a panic. They came to Moses and told him that Pharaoh's chariots were nearly on top of them. Moses, however, did not panic. He was not fearful. Instead, we read in Exodus 14:13, "And Moses said unto the people, 'Fear ye not, stand still, and see the salvation of the LORD, which he will show to you to day: for the Egyptians whom you have seen today, ye shall see them again no more for ever.'" Since he knew God, because he was a man of God, he did not fear the Egyptians; he did not fear the world. Instead, he took the light of the Lord and in the midst of trials and adversity he could "…stand still, and see the salvation of the Lord…"

The first five books of the Bible were written by Moses; the last being the book of Deuteronomy. Moses wrote the entire book of Deuteronomy on his one hundred, twentieth birthday, the last day that he had to live.

I have often wondered what I would do in the same setting. If God told me that I had one day to live, how would I live it? Would I spend as much time with my family as I could? Would I spend time getting my affairs in order? Would I draft a will? Would I eat my favorite meal or go fishing or hunting, which to me are my favorite avocations? Or would I be like Moses, a man of God, who spent his last day on earth serving the Lord by writing the book of Deuteronomy as God had commanded him to do?

In Exodus chapter 33, verses 1–3 we read, "And the Lord said unto Moses, 'Depart, and go up hence, thou and the people which thou hast brought up out of the land of Egypt, unto the land which I sware unto Abraham, to Isaac, and to Jacob, saying, Unto thy seed will I give it: And I will send an angel before thee; and I will drive out the Canaanite, the Amorite and the Hittite, and the Perizzite, and the Hivite, and the Jebusite: Unto a land flowing with milk and honey: for I will not go up in the midst of thee; for thou art a stiffnecked people: lest I consume thee in the way.'" God told Moses to take the people to the land He had promised them, the very land they had waited hundreds of years to inherit. God even promised Moses that He would send an angel to accompany them.

However, to Moses, this was not sufficient. He would not go without God, his friend. His heart yearned for God more than the Promised Land, more than the promises which God had given him and his people. "And he said unto him, 'If thy presence go not with me, carry us not up hence'" (Exod. 33:15, KJV). Moses would rather have stayed in the wilderness, the desert, amid much discomfort with God's presence, than go to the Promised Land flowing with milk and honey without God's presence.

To Moses, the Promised Land was nothing without God's presence. He refused God's offer even though it would have resulted in a much more comfortable life. His cry was only that he may know God and be in His presence.

Moses loved God for who God was. The Israelites loved God for what He could do for them. John Bevere writes, "Moses and

Israel perfectly illustrate the two groups of people that make up the church today. This fundamental difference is the dividing line in the church, which reveals the genuine worshippers and those who profess Jesus as Lord, yet are self-seeking" (*A Heart Ablaze*, 78).

Moses spent more time in the presence of God than any other person in his day. He also delighted himself in serving God more than any other. As such, God called him a faithful servant: "My servant Moses is not so, who is faithful in all mine house" (Num. 12:7, KJV).

Moses was one of the two that God called a man of God, the other being Elijah (II Kings 1:10, KJV). God recognized what His relationship with Moses was and labeled Moses as such. In Deuteronomy 33:1 we read, "And this is the blessing, wherewith Moses the man of God blessed the children of Israel before his death."

Andrew Murray in *Daily Experience with God*, describes this as the following: "'The *man of God*! How much this name means! He is a man who comes from God, chosen and sent by Him. He walks with God, lives in His fellowship, and carries the mark of His presence. He is a man who lives for God and His will. His whole being is ruled by the glory of God, and he involuntarily and unceasingly causes men to think of God. In his heart the life of God is taking its rightful place as the all in all. His one desire is that God should have that place of prominence in men's hearts throughout the world" (Chapter 6).

To be a man or woman of God is what the world needs now. God seeks these individuals so that He may fill them with Himself and send them into the world to help others to know Him. A person can give himself completely to the presence of the Holy Spirit, not only as a power working in him, but also as God dwelling in him. And he can become, in the deepest meaning of the word, a "man of God" (John 14:16, 20, 23; I John 4:13–16, KJV).

Andrew Murray continues with the following exhortation, which I echo:

> Brother and sister, seek to be a man or woman of God! Let God be all to you in the morning watch. Let God be all to you during the day. And let your life be devoted to one thing—to bring men to God, and God to men. Let it be your desire that, in His church and in the world, God may have the place due to Him. Turn back now and look at Moses, the man of prayer and of the Word. See how Moses grew out of these to be the man of God. See the way in which it becomes divinely possible to be and live as a man or woman of God. Then study how you can apply these lessons to your own life.

Indeed, let us all aspire to be a man of God as Moses was!

TO BE A MAN OF GOD LIKE MOSES—
THE WORK OF THE CROSS

And he said, "Thou canst not see my face: for there shall
no man see me, and live" (Exod. 33:20, KJV). And there
arose not a prophet since in Israel like unto Moses, whom
the Lord knew face to face, In all the signs and the wonders,
which the Lord sent him to do in the land of Egypt
to Pharaoh, and to all his servant, and to all his land.

—D EUT. 34:10–12, KJV

We have learned that Moses was a man of God (Deut. 33:1, KJV). This is the fourth step in being made whole in the eyes of God. We touched on many of the facets of Moses' life that allowed him to be called a man of God. However, this step embraces the most important thing in our walk with God after our salvation. This step is the work of the cross in us.

There are four steps in the development of a believer. The first step is salvation. The second step is the Baptism of the Holy Spirit. The Baptism of the Holy Spirit is not necessary for salvation as some have taught. However, it is a separate event. It represents an infilling of the Holy Spirit just as the disciples received in the Upper Room. It is not necessary for our salvation, but it is necessary for our service for God and for the power of God to be worked through us. With the Baptism of the Holy Spirit, we receive the gifts of the Holy Spirit. The third step is the work of the cross. The final step is the resurrection life. Just as Jesus had life after He passed through death on the cross, so too, will we. That is where we will receive the fullness of God. That is when we will be whole.

It is therefore possible for Spirit-filled believers to be very carnal, and I am sure unfortunately, that we all know examples of individuals like this. How is this possible? How can you not only have the Spirit of God living in you, which is the measure of the Spirit that is given to all people at their conversion and furthermore the Baptism of the Holy Spirit, yet be carnal? It is because these individuals do not go on and complete step three, which is the work of the cross.

To be a man or woman of God, you must embrace the cross, and you must have its work in you. Moses knew this and furthermore, Moses embraced it.

Moses, as with each of us, was chosen by God for his role before he was created. In Exodus 1:22 we read that the Egyptian Pharaoh decreed that every Israeli son that was born would be killed by being cast into the river. In the second chapter of Exodus, we read of the birth and deliverance of Moses from the Pharaoh's decree. Both of Moses' parents were from the tribe of

Levi. This was the tribe that God would set apart for His priests. The entire tribe of Levi would be set apart to serve Him. After Moses' birth, his mother could immediately see "…that he was a goodly child…" (Exod. 2:2, KJV). When she could no longer hide him, she put him in an ark and floated it down the river. There, the daughter of Pharaoh found and saved him. Moses' mother was allowed to nurse him. After Moses had grown, his mother brought him to the Pharaoh's daughter and he became the Pharaoh's daughter's son. It was she who named him Moses.

Moses knew what his ultimate call would be. He knew that he was to lead his fellow Israelites out of Egypt. He tried to do it his way, however only God's way works. When he saw an Egyptian beating one of his Hebrew brethren and thought that no one was looking, he killed the Egyptian and buried him in the sand. He thought the Israelites would rally behind him, but they did not. When Pharaoh sought to slay Moses, he fled into the desert (Exodus, chapter 2, KJV).

Moses was in the wilderness, the desert, for forty years. All of us will have at least one wilderness experience. Most of us will have more than one. Hopefully, ours will not be of a forty-year duration as was Moses'. It is during these wilderness times that God transforms us into His image and likeness. It is during these times that He removes ourself from ourselves. It is during these times that we have a major work of the cross performed in us.

After Paul's conversion, he went to the desert, the wilderness, for three years. He went to the exact same spot that Moses did.

Paul was then taken to the third heaven where he received untold revelations from God. He then had another fourteen-year wilderness experience before he began his ministry. Thus, we should not think it strange when we enter into a wilderness experience. Rather, we should ask God to transform us. We should ask Him what we are to learn from this experience so that we may pass through it quickly and move on.

However, there was a difference in Moses' wilderness experience. God did not call Moses into the wilderness as He called Paul and as He will call each of us who are serious about serving Him. No, Moses did this on his own. He birthed this Ishmael. Moses had to get to the point where he placed his own Ishmael on the altar for sacrifice. God did not tell him to kill the Egyptian. God did not tell him to flee into the wilderness. God told Paul to go to the wilderness, but Moses did this on his own. That is why it took a forty-year wilderness experience for Moses.

We should learn from this. We can do things which we feel are good for the Kingdom. We can even volunteer to go to the wilderness. But, unless God has ordained these things for us and asked us to do them, they will be of our own accord and not His. We will be birthing Ishmaels then as well.

After Moses had completed his wilderness experience, God came to him as a fire in a burning bush, which did not consume the bush, and called him. There, God gave him his calling and commission. There, he charged Moses to deliver the Israelites.

It is worth looking at how God called Moses. In Exodus 3:2–3 we read, "And the angel of the LORD appeared unto him in a flame of fire out of the midst of a bush: and he looked, and, behold, the bush burned with fire, and the bush was not consumed. And Moses said, 'I will now turn aside, and see this great sight, why the bush is not burnt.'" In the Old Testament, the angel of the Lord is Jesus. Jesus Himself appeared unto Moses. So too, will Jesus appear to us at our calling and commission. It may not be as a visible sign as it was with Moses, but we will know it is from the Lord. God always gives us a choice, however. Here He gave Moses a choice. He asks us always to choose Him and life over death in all that we do. When we receive our call and commission from God, we have a choice to accept or not. Jesus appeared to Moses in the burning bush. Moses had a choice to go and see Him or not. Moses made the correct choice. He said "…I will now turn aside, and see this great sight…" (Exod. 3:3, KJV).

Why is this important? It was only after Moses went that God spoke to Him. If we draw nigh to God, God will draw nigh to us (James 4:8, KJV). When Moses turned aside to see God, to pursue Him, then God responded and spoke to Moses (Exod. 3:4, KJV).

Moses was initially reluctant to obey God and fulfill the call of God that was placed on his life (Exodus, chapter 4, KJV). However, once he had passed this, he was never fearful again.

Moses then took his family and journeyed to Egypt to fulfill the Lord's call that God had given him. In what is one of the most intriguing verses in the Scripture, we read in Exodus 4:24 the following: "And it came to pass by the way in the inn, that the Lord met him, and sought to kill him." God had given Moses his call and commission, and had equipped him for service which God will always do. The Lord will never ask us to do anything without giving us the means to do it. Moses was reluctant, but eventually accepted his call and went forth. Then we read as he was going forth to complete the call and commission that God had given him, fearlessly, the Lord met him on his journey and "...sought to kill him." Why? It is because Moses was not obedient to God's previous commands. God does not feel it is necessary to repeat the commands that He has given us before. We are responsible for knowing and complying with what He has told and taught us. Moses knew that he was to have circumcised his son, yet he did not. He did not hold up his end of the blood covenant that God had given to Abraham. This is why God "sought to kill him." Fortunately, Moses' wife, Zipporah, knew the law better than Moses did. She realized what had happened. She realized the source of the Lord's anger, and she immediately performed the circumcision on her son. God's anger was abated and Moses was allowed to continue on his journey. We must remember to keep the commands that the Lord has given us.

Moses then accomplished many things and was mighty in a way that few other men have ever been used by God. Egypt stands for the world and satan's kingdom. The Israelite's exodus stands for their salvation, and the crossing of the Red Sea their water baptism. The Pharaoh was the most powerful person in the world. In a way, he could be considered to be the ancient equivalent of the anti-Christ which shall come. Yet, Moses fearlessly obeyed God and went into the Pharaoh's presence, knowing that his life was in jeopardy for doing so. There, God used him as His vessel to perform the miracles that Moses did. God used him to enter the enemy's camp itself and defeat the enemy there. Moses understood God. When all the Israelites were in fear as the Egyptians approached them and they were pinned against the Red Sea, Moses could command them by saying, "And Moses said unto the people, 'Fear ye not, stand still, and see the salvation of the LORD, which he will show to you to day: for the Egyptians whom you have seen to day, ye shall see them again no more for ever'" (Exod. 14:13, KJV).

Moses was many things. He was the meekest man who ever lived (Num. 12:3, KJV). He was the greatest prophet (Deut. 34:10, KJV). He was a "man of God" (Deut. 33:1; Josh. 14:6; I Chron. 23:14; Ezra 3:2, KJV). Moses knew the Lord face to face (Deut. 34:10, KJV). Moses was also called a friend of God. As we reviewed in the last chapter, Moses, like Joseph, had become a prayer. His prayer life was extraordinary. His prayer life was one that could happen only when one is truly intimate with God.

Moses did much more. There are only three people who fasted for forty days. The other two were Elijah and Jesus Himself. Moses did it twice. Twice for forty days he was in the presence of God on top of the mountain. There, God sustained him supernaturally, because he ate directly from the tree of life. He ate from the hand of God Himself. Even after the exodus, God used Moses in a mighty way. He performed many miracles and wonders. He defeated the enemy countless times. He was the leader of God's chosen people.

Moses always knew where to find God. He had a secret place.

He placed his tent outside the congregation. There he met with God, and the Israelites knew this (Exod. 33:7–11, KJV). Moses spoke to God and said he would not go and lead his people if God did not go with him. He had to have God's presence. God honored his request and agreed to go with him.

Therefore, there is no dispute that God used Moses in a mighty way. I personally know no one who has accomplished this or has the relationship with God that Moses had at this point in his life. I know no one who in their prayer life, has the relationship with God that Moses had at this point in his life. I believe that if most of us were at this place in our walk with God and were being used by God in this way, we would be content, thankful and satisfied.

Moses, however, was not. Moses wanted more. He understood what Paul wrote when he said, "I press on to the mark of the high calling of God" (Phil. 3:14, KJV). Moses was not satisfied to be where he was, even though it was where no one had ever been before. No, Moses pressed on.

In Exodus 33:17–23 we read, "And the Lord said unto Moses, 'I will do this thing also that thou hast spoken: for thou hast found grace in my sight, and I know thee by name.' And he said, 'I beseech thee, show me thy glory.' And he said, 'I will make all my goodness pass before thee, and I will proclaim the name of the LORD before thee; and will be gracious to whom I will be gracious, and will show mercy on whom I will show mercy.' And he said, 'Thou canst not see my face: for there shall no man see me, and live.' And the LORD said, 'Behold, there is a place by me, and thou shalt stand upon a rock: And it shall come to pass, while my glory passeth by, that I will put thee in a clift of the rock, and will cover thee with my hand while I pass by: And I will take away mine hand, and thou shalt see my back parts: but my face shall not be seen.'" Moses was not satisfied where he was. He wanted more. He did not just want the hand of God. He did not want just the promises of God. The Israelites were content with that, but Moses was not. He had been on top of the mountain. He had been in the presence of God. He had tasted and eaten directly from the tree of life. He was not satiated or satisfied. He wanted more. He said, "God I will not go forth unless you go with me. I must have Your presence. And God, even though I know You at this level, show me Your glory. Show me more of You. Show me Yourself, so that I may truly know You, that I may truly know Your face."

God's answer was somewhat unsettling. Even though Moses was at a relationship level with God that no one else had been before, he still could not stand before God. God told him, "No, Moses you cannot behold My glory. You cannot see Me face to face. No man can see Me face to face and live. What I will do for you though Moses, is put you in the cleft of the rock, the rock of Jesus." God said, "Moses, you cannot see Me face to face. You cannot see Me because you are not ready to behold Me. If you were to see Me now, you would die. So, you can see Me through Jesus. Jesus will put you into His bosom, the cleft of the rock. Then I will pass by. As I pass by, I will cover your face with My hand. After I pass by, I will remove my hand, and you will be able to see My backside; however, you will not be able to see My face."

In the last chapter of Deuteronomy we read, "And there arose not a prophet since in Israel like unto Moses, whom the Lord knew face to face, In all the signs and the wonders, which the Lord sent him to do in the land of Egypt to Pharaoh, and to all his servants, and to all his land, And in all that mighty hand, and in all the great terror which Moses shewed in the sight of all Israel" (Deut. 34:10–12, KJV). In these verses we see that Moses did know God face to face.

Returning to Exodus 33, God told Moses that he could not see His face. He could not see Him face to face because no man who was alive could see Him and live. However, in Deuteronomy 34:10 we read Moses did know Him face to face. Therefore, something happened in between. Something happened that allowed Moses to go into the presence of the Lord and see Him face to face and live. What was this? It was the work of the cross in Moses. Therefore, to become a man of God one has to have the completion of the work of the cross in himself.

It is true that no one who is alive can see God in Heaven. No flesh shall glory in the presence of God. To come into the presence of God, we must become pure and chaste. God is holy, and nothing that is unholy can come into His presence. Moses understood this. So too, should we. The closer we are to God, the more pure and chaste we have to be. The closer we are to the glory and the manifest presence of God, the more swift and severe is the judgment of God.

Moses understood there is but one way to behold God's face. There is just one way to know God face to face. There is only one way to go into His presence and behold the beauty and glory of God. What is this way? The cross. It is the work of the cross. It always comes back to the cross. Through the work of the cross, we die to self. When you are dead, you cannot die again. When you are dead to self, when your self is not alive, when you have died to self and exist just to do God's will and good pleasure, then you can come into His presence and live; then and only then.

We read of the work of the cross and the key to Moses dying to self in Exodus 34:29–35. These verses read:

> And it came to pass, when Moses came down from Mount Sinai with the two tables of testimony in Moses' hand, when he came down from the mount, that Moses wist not that the skin of his face shone while he talked with him. And when Aaron and all the children of Israel saw Moses, behold, the skin of his face shone; and they were afraid to come nigh him. And Moses called unto them; and Aaron and all the rulers of the congregation returned unto him: and Moses talked with them. And afterward all the children of Israel came nigh: and he gave them in commandment all that the Lord had spoken with him in Mount Sinai. And till Moses had done speaking with them, he put a veil on his face. But when Moses went in before the Lord to speak with him, he took the veil off, until he came out. And he came out, and spake unto the

children of Israel that which he was commanded. And the children of Israel saw the face of Moses, that the skin of Moses' face shone: and Moses put the veil upon his face again, until he went in to speak with him.

When we are in the presence of God, just like Moses, when we behold our Lord's glory, that glory extends to us. We take it with us wherever we go. People see that glory. This is the light of God that Paul wrote about in Ephesians. We do not have to say a word. The light of God, the glory of God that is upon us after we are in His presence, pushes the darkness back. The world knows. The world sees it. To those who are in darkness, it is uncomfortable. It convicts them. They do not want to see it. They ask us to cover up our face as well. They ask us not to speak about Jesus. They ask us to do as they do. So it was with Moses. When he came out of the presence of God, the Lord's glory was upon him. It made the Israelites uncomfortable, and they asked him to put a veil over his face when he was in their midst. However, when Moses went back into the presence of God, he removed his veil.

What does this veil represent? It is the veil that we all have. It does not cover our face, but our heart. It is the part of the world that we have that we do not want to give up, or it is the part of the world that we do not even know about. All of us have darkness in our heart that we may or may not know about. God does not look on the outside like we do. He looks on the inside. He looks at the heart. God wants us to hold nothing back. He has asked us to give Him all of ourselves. Moses understood this. When he went into the presence of God, he removed his veil. He exposed himself to God, and he asked God to deal with it. He asked God to remove that part of him. This was the dying of self. This was the work of the cross in Moses.

God will settle for nothing less for us. We can hold nothing back from God. We must reveal all to Him. We must yield all. We must remove the veil from our hearts and ask God to remove the darkness from us, including that which we know and do not know about. Saints, this was the key for Moses.

God asks us always to pursue Him. As long as we seek Him first, we eat from Him and the Tree of Life. Moses understood this. He continued to pursue the Living Water. He continued to pursue God. There is a valuable lesson to be learned from this in Moses. Moses had accomplished many things and could have stopped and been content with what he had. He may have even had a right to do that. Fortunately, he did not. He pressed on. If he had stopped, God would have continued to use him where he was. He would have still been used in a magnificent way, for the giftings and callings of God are irrevocable (Rom. 11:29, KJV). But, he did not stop there.

Paul knew this. Paul wrote that he had to press on to the mark of the high calling in Christ Jesus. This is pressing on to the completion of Christ in us and us in Him. It is pressing on to become all that God wants us to be. Paul wrote that he counted all things as dung, except the knowledge of Christ and Him crucified. This is all things. All things include worldly things. For some this is hard to give up. That is why rich successful people in the world do not come to accept Christ as easily as others. Jesus Himself stated that it is easier for a camel to get through the eye of the needle than a rich man to come into the Kingdom of God (Matt. 19:24, KJV). Paul had everything in the world, but he knew that all these things were not important, and he gave them up. So too, must we.

Giving up the things of the world is easy when we receive and see the life of Jesus. The hard part is giving up the Kingdom things that we have acquired after our conversion. This is the true component of what Paul was writing about when he wrote that he counted all things as dung except the knowledge of Christ and Him crucified. All things include spiritual things just like worldly things.

"Remember Lot's wife" (Luke 17:32, KJV). Lot's wife looked back and died as a result. So too, will we, if we look back. We may not die physically, but we will die spiritually. Paul wrote that there is no such thing as standing still. We are either moving forward or backwards. We must learn this lesson from Moses and Paul. We can never be content where we are. God always has more for us. When we reach a certain plateau in the Kingdom, we can be satisfied. From my own experience, I can say it is a wonderful thing when the Lord uses me as He does. When He gives me a revelation, word or teaching, it is an incredible feeling. I could be content to stop here, and God will continue to use me in this capacity. But, that is not what He wants. Paul and Moses understood that. As long as we pursue Jesus, as long as we eat from the Tree of Life, as long as we drink from the Living Water, as long as we go deep into the well of the Living Water into Jesus, then we press on. God will still use us for the giftings, calls and commissions that He has given us, only He will use them in us in a greater way if we continue to pursue Him and eat of the Tree of Life. If we ever become satisfied, we stop. We stop because we eat of the tree of knowledge.

As we have discussed, Moses accomplished many, many things that few of us will ever see or even dream possible. He could have easily been satisfied, but he was not. He wanted more of God. He knew that there was more of God that he could obtain. He desired and sought after them. He counted all things as dung that the Lord had used him for, and he pressed on. As much as he had accomplished, he still could not behold God face to face, and he wanted to. He remembered Lot's wife and did not look back. Rather, he pressed on to the mark of the high calling. Saints, let us learn this lesson as well.

There are many things that happened between Exodus chapter 33, where Moses asked God to let him see His glory, and God told him no, and Deuteronomy chapter 34, where we read that Moses knew God face to face. One thing that did happen was that Moses built a tabernacle. He built a dwelling place for God. So too, must we, if we want to become a man of God. So too, must we, if we want to know God. So too, must we, if we want to see and know God face to face. The dwelling place of God now is us. He resides in our heart. He resides in our inner man. The current temple of God is us. God has given us a Promised Land, but He has a Promised Land as well. We, His chosen, His redeemed, are His Promised Land. Just like we need to desire and go forth and possess our Promised Land, so too, does God desire to possess His Promised Land. Moses removed the veil from his heart when he went into the presence of God. By doing so, he prepared his dwelling place for God, and God could go into His Promised Land in Moses.

There are only two things to seek for, writes Francis Frangipane: 1) To know the heart of God in Christ; and 2) to know our own heart in Christ's light. The truth is knowing God's heart as it is revealed in Christ. And it is knowing our own hearts in the light of God's grace. When we search for God's heart, we are also searching for our own heart, for it is only in finding Him that we discover ourselves. It is only in finding Him that we are in Him.

God is seeking those that want this intimate relationship with Him. He must have them; He must have the remnant for the great end-time harvest. We read in Psalms 53:2, "God looked down from heaven upon the children of men, to see if there were any that did understand, that did seek God." He is looking down upon His children, those that He has chosen and redeemed, to see if there is a remnant. He is looking at us now to see if any of us understand what He is asking us to do. He is looking at His bride, His church, to see if any are seeking Him, truly seeking Him face to face. Truly seeking Him face to face not for their own good, but for His name's sake, glory and benefit only.

One man with this quality of heart captures the attention and promise of God. "For all those things hath mine hand made, and all those things had been saith the Lord: but to this man will I look, even to him that is poor and of a contrite spirit and trembleth at my word" (Isa. 66:2, KJV). To this man who truly seeks God, God will look. Deuteronomy 4:29 reads, "But if from thence thou shalt seek the LORD thy God, thou shalt find him, if thou seek him with all thy heart and with all thy soul." This is the key. To know Him face to face, to become Christ conscious and to lose all self-consciousness, we must seek Him with all our heart and with all our soul.

Concerning this aspect of Moses and the work of the cross in him, Andrew Murray in *The Path to Holiness* writes as follows:

Only under the influence of a high spiritual elevation and joy can God's holiness be fully apprehended or rightly worshipped. The sentiment that becomes us as we worship the Holy One, it fits us for knowing and worshipping Him aright, is a spirit of praise that sings and shouts for joy in the experience of His full salvation.

But does this contradict the lesson we learned at Horeb, when God said, "Do not come any closer...Take off your sandals" (Exod. 3:5, KJV), and where Moses feared and hid his face? Is hiding our face not the fitting attitude for us as creatures and sinners? Yes, it is. But the two sentiments are not contradictory; rather they are indispensable to each other. The fear is the preparation for the praise and the glory. Is it not the same Moses who hid his face in fear to look upon God, who afterward beheld His glory until his own face shone with a brightness that men could not bear to look upon? Is not this song that speaks of God as glorious and holiness also the song of Moses who feared and hid his face? Have we not seen in the fire and in God—especially in His holiness—a twofold aspect: consuming and purifying, repelling and attracting, judging and saving? In each case the latter is not only the accompaniment but also the result of the former.

As I look upon the two sides of His holiness, as revealed to the Egyptians and the Israelites, I remember that what was there separated is in me united. By nature I am the Egyptian, an enemy doomed to destruction; by grace, an Israelite chosen for redemption. In me the fire must consume and destroy; only as judgment does its work can mercy fully save. It is only as I tremble before the searching light, the burning fire, the consuming heat of the Holy One, as I yield my Egyptian nature to be judged, condemned, and slain, that the Israelite will be redeemed to know His God as the God of salvation and to rejoice in Him.

Praise God! The judgment is passed. In Christ, the burning bush, the fire of the divine holiness has done its double work. In Him sin was condemned in the flesh, in Him we are free. In giving up His will to death and doing God's will, Christ sanctified Himself, and in that will we are sanctified too. His crucifixion was its judgment of the flesh. His death with its entire putting off of what is natural is not only for us, but is, in fact, ours—a life and power working within us by His Spirit. Day by day we abide in Him with fear and trembling, but we rejoice and we take our stand in Him. The power of holiness as judgment against sin and flesh allows it to accomplish its glorious work. We give thanks at the remembrance of His holiness. So the shout of salvation rings ever deeper, truer, and louder throughout life: "Who is like you—majestic in holiness, awesome in glory, working wonders?" (Used with permission from Baker Publishing Group, all rights reserved: Andrew Murray, *The Path to Holiness* [Grand Rapids: Bethany House, a division of Baker Publishing Group, 1984], 50–52.)

God is no respecter of a person. That is why I enjoy reading about the accounts of men in the Bible. If all the great things in the Bible were accomplished by Jesus only, we could say that it was because He was Jesus. When we read of men like Moses and what they accomplished, we know that it is God's intent for the same for us. God wants each of us to be a man of God. God wants each of us to be His dwelling place and Promised Land. God wants each of us to go from seeking Him, but not being able to come into His presence, because nothing that is alive can see His face and live, to knowing Him face to face. This is His desire. It is possible. So too, should it be our desire. There is one way and one way only. Moses' life personified this. Once again, it is the work of the cross. With Moses it was seen by the removal of the veil from his face and heart. By doing so, he allowed God to perform the necessary work in him so that he could become pure and chaste enough to go into the presence of God. Let us aspire to be like Moses. Let us aspire and become a man of God that knows God face to face, and go into the fullness of God's presence any time we want. And when we return into the world, we will then carry the light and glory of God. The world will see and know it without a word being spoken. Then the darkness is defeated and our enemy is destroyed!

Indeed, as Oswald Chambers wrote in *My Utmost For His Highest,* "'...after Moses was grown...he went out to his brethren and looked at their burdens' (Exod. 2:11, KJV). In the beginning, Moses had realized that he was the one to deliver the people, but he had to be trained and disciplined by God first. He was right in his individual perspective, but he was not the person for the work until he had learned true fellowship and oneness with God." This included a dying out to his own agenda and taking on God's purposes.

STEP FIVE:
TO HAVE THE HEART OF GOD AS DAVID

For it came to pass, when Solomon was old,
that his wives turned away his heart after other gods:
and his heart was not perfect with the LORD
his God as was the heart of David his father.

—I KINGS 11:4, KJV

A s great as Moses was and as great as being a man of God like Moses is, we must not be content. We must press on as Moses himself did. We must press on to the next level in our walk with God, and that is to have the heart of God as David did. If you are a man of God, then you can have the heart of God that David had.

David fell short and sinned. David's sins were grievous ones. In I Chronicles 21:1 and II Samuel 24:1 we read where God allowed satan to tempt David for evil. This was to find out what was indeed in David's heart. Unfortunately, David failed this test. God had worked mighty military victories and miracles through David and allowed David to rule as King. God wanted David to continue to rely on Him and not himself. But, when David failed this test, rather than relying on God he ordered his military men to be numbered. In other words, he did a census of his country to see how big his army was. This was against the advice of his advisors who knew that he should not be doing it. Nevertheless, he did, and God judged him and the Israelites greatly. "And God was displeased with this thing; therefore he smote Israel" (I Chron. 21:7, KJV).

David's adultery with Bathsheba is well-known (II Samuel, chapter 11, KJV). Bathsheba was married, but this did not stop David's lust for her. He took and committed adultery with her, and she became pregnant with his child. As a result, he plotted and eventually arranged for the murder of her husband, Uriah the Hittite. Certainly this was an evil thing and "…the thing that David had done displeased the LORD" (II Samuel 11:27, KJV). Furthermore, David did not repent of this sin until the Lord sent the prophet Nathan to David. Then the Lord, through Nathan, confronted David with his sin (II Samuel, chapter 12, KJV). As a result, the Lord punished David, and the child that was born of the adulterous relationship before David married Bathsheba, died.

It was because of this that David was not allowed to build the temple. David's heart was for God. As such, he longed to build God a home. He communed with God when others did not. Therefore, he wanted to build a home for God where he and others could come and worship God. God would not allow him to do so. God gave him the plans and the means to build the temple, but God would not allow him to build the temple. Rather, David and Bathsheba's son, Solomon, built the temple.

However, in spite of his shortcomings, and all of us have had our own, he still loved God with all his heart. God rewarded him because God recognized this. David's heart was after God's heart. David had the heart of God.

It did not begin this way though. David's heart was beating its own beat with its separate rhythm, which was different from the beat and rhythm of God's heart. Eventually, by yielding himself to the Master, David's heart rate was changed to coincide with that of God's. Eventually, they were beating in perfect synchrony and harmony, finally uniting, infused together as one. David then had God's heart.

In what is referred to as the great commandment, Jesus said that the greatest thing we should do was to love God with all our heart. "Jesus said unto him, 'Thou shalt love the Lord thy God with all thy heart, and with all thy soul, and with all thy mind'" (Matt. 22:37, KJV). When we have God's heart, then we can begin to have His love. When we begin to have His love, then we can love one another as He has loved us.

To have the heart of God, we must seek Him. Not only must we seek Him, but we must seek Him passionately. God has told us this repeatedly. He has promised us that if we seek Him, we will find Him, but the key to this is we must seek Him with our entire heart and being. In Deuteronomy 4:29 we read, "But if from thence thou shalt seek the Lord thy God, thou shalt find him, if thou seek him with all thy heart, and with all thy soul." Jeremiah 29:13 states the same and reads, "And ye shall seek me, and find me, when ye shall search for me with all your heart."

David knew this. He sought God. He wanted nothing else. When the Lord told him this, he answered, "When thou saidst, Seek ye my face; my heart said unto thee, Thy face, LORD, will I seek" (Ps. 27:8, KJV).

God rewardeth those such as Ezra who had a heart after God and sought Him. "For Ezra had prepared his heart to seek the law of the Lord, and to do it, and to teach in Israel statutes and judgments" (Ezra 7:10, KJV). Likewise, those like Rehoboam did evil because they did not seek God with their heart. "And he did evil, because he prepared not his heart to seek the LORD" (II Chron. 12:14, KJV).

To seek God, we must hunger for Him. We must truly hunger for Him over everything else. David did, and that is why he had the heart of God. David could truly say, "As the deer panteth after the water brooks, so panteth my soul after thee, O God" (Ps. 42:1, KJV). Furthermore, he stated this: "One thing have I desired of the LORD, that will I seek after; that I may dwell in the house of the LORD all the days of my life, to behold the beauty of the Lord, and to inquire in his temple" (Ps. 27:4, KJV). To dwell in the house of the Lord means to be in His presence. David longed to be with God. That is what his heart desired, so he sought this. He wanted to be with the Lord. He wanted to be in the Lord's presence. Not just sometimes, not just occasionally, but all the time. When you are in the presence of the Lord, you can behold His beauty. You see Him face to face, and you can inquire of Him. There, God will give you revelation of Himself.

David hungered for God. In Matthew 12:3 we read what

Jesus said about this. This verse reads, "But he said unto them, 'Have ye not read what David did, when he was an hungered, and they that were with him?'"

If you were to ask someone if it was possible to be perfect, the immediate overwhelming answer is no, as there was only one perfect One and that was Jesus. However, this is not true. God has commanded us to be perfect. "Thou shalt be perfect with the Lord thy God" (Deut. 18:13, KJV). "Be ye therefore perfect even as your father which is in heaven is perfect" (Matt. 5:48, KJV). The Bible declares that four people were, in fact, perfect: Noah, King Asa, Job and David. To be perfect does not mean to be perfected. To be perfect in God's eyes means to have a perfect heart before Him. It means to have God's heart. To be perfect in God's eyes means we must love God more than anything else, and be totally and absolutely submissive to His will. We must place God's will over our own will. David did this. Thus, he had God's heart. Acts 13:22 reads, "And when he had removed him, he raised up their King; to whom also he gave testimony, and said, 'I have found David the son of Jesse, a man after mine own heart, which shall fulfill all my will.'"

When we develop the heart of God, we will know God. We will know His will and ways immediately without having to ask or even think about it.

To have the heart of God is what Tommy Tenney's ministry is all about. His ministry is to exhort us to be a God Chaser. This is one who has the heart of God.

You develop the heart of God through seeking Him and

being a worshipper. Worship is the key. This is what David wrote in Psalms 149. Here he exhorted himself and us to praise the Lord, sing a new song to Him, and praise Him when alone or with others, with dance and music. However, we choose to do so or not. Therefore, we must choose and make the effort to praise and worship the Lord.

To have the heart of God and to seek Him and do His will, we must lose self-consciousness and obtain total Christ consciousness. We do this by seeking Jesus in all that we do. We must not just seek His touch, and we must not just seek Him for ourselves. We must learn to go beyond that. We must seek Jesus for Him. We must seek Him for His good will and pleasure. We must seek Him face to face. We must empty ourselves of ourselves. We indeed must lose self-consciousness. We can come into His presence not for our sake, but purely for His sake, seeking His face, not His hand, only by losing self-consciousness. This allows us to gain Christ-consciousness.

To have the heart of God…It is possible, and it is our Lord's desire for each of us. As a man and King, David fell short. He did not stay there though. He was also a champion. He got up and recovered after he fell instead of staying where he was. David sinned, but he was perfect in the eyes of God. He was perfect in the eyes of God because He had a heart after God's own heart. He longed for God. He sought God. He sought God passionately. He hungered for God. He delighted in doing God's will. As Tommy Tenney stated, "Many people want to enjoy the blessings of the Kingdom without getting close to the King. It doesn't happen that way. As we seek and draw near to the heart of the King, our own hearts will be satisfied. The Psalmist wrote, 'Delight thyself also in the LORD; and he shall give thee the desires of thine heart. Commit thy way unto the LORD; trust also in him; and he shall bring it to pass' (Ps. 37:4–5, KJV). We desire what we delight in. And our greatest desire will be for Him!"

"God rewards those who seek Him. Not those who seek doctrine or religion or systems or creeds. Many settle for these lesser passions, but the reward goes to those who settle for nothing less than Jesus Himself. And what is the reward? What awaits those who seek Jesus? Nothing short of the heart of Jesus." (Max Lucado, *Just Like Jesus*)

Let us, like David, aspire for and develop a heart after God. Let us have God's heart. Let us be considered perfect in the eyes of God!

chapter nine

STEP SIX:
TO HAVE THE LOVE OF GOD AS JOHN

Now there was leaning on Jesus' bosom
one of his disciples, whom Jesus loved.

—JOHN 13:23, KJV

E ven though we should all aspire to have the heart of God as David did, there is more. There is another level to progress to. This next level in our maturation, in our walk with God, is to have the love of God as John did.

While they were celebrating the Passover Feast, at the Last Supper Jesus told the twelve apostles that one would betray Him (John 13:18–19, KJV). Furthermore, we read in John 13:21, "When Jesus had thus said, he was troubled in his spirit, and testifieth, and said, 'Verily, verily, I say unto you, that one of you shall betray me.'"

This, of course, troubled the disciples. They had been together serving Jesus during His entire three and one-half year earthly ministry. Surely one of them would not betray Him and thus the others as well. Yet, Jesus the Master said so. I can only imagine the emotions they were feeling. Some were unsure and were asking themselves if they were the one that was going to betray Jesus. Others were busy looking around at the other eleven accusing first one and then another. Many were deeply troubled. Some were angry and others sad. All were upset and deeply moved by what Jesus had told them. We read of this in the next verse, John 13:22, which reads, "Then the disciples looked one on another, doubting of whom he spake."

What therefore did they do? It was the custom at that time when one ate not to sit on chairs at a table. Rather, one would lie on cushions. Evidently, John was lying next to Jesus. After an unsettling period of time had passed, we read that John leaned over to Jesus. This is given to us in John 13:23, which reads, "Now there was leaning on Jesus' bosom one of his disciples, whom Jesus loved." John frequently described himself in the gospel he wrote as the one whom Jesus loved.

Ostensibly, John did this to learn who the traitor would be. In John 13:24–25 we read, "Simon Peter therefore beckoned to him, that he should ask who it should be of whom he spake. He then lying on Jesus' breast saith unto him, 'Lord, Who is it?'" The Lord then revealed it to all, for in verse 26 we read, "Jesus answered, 'He it is, to whom I shall give a sop {this morsel (RSV)}, when I have dipped it.' And when he dipped the sop, he gave it to Judas Iscariot, the son of Simon."

Immediately after this, satan himself entered into Judas. Jesus told Judas to leave, and he did. This is given to us in John 13:27, which reads, "And after the sop satan entered him. Then said Jesus unto him, 'That thou doest, do quickly.'"

It is interesting that Jesus did not hide this. He clearly told John what He was going to do and that the one He gave the bread dipped in wine to would be the one who would betray Him. However, as was often the case, even though this was meant to be for all the disciples, not all of them paid attention nor took notice. Indeed, in John 13:28 we read, "Now no man at the table knew for what intent he spake this unto him." Continuing in verse 29 we read, "For some of them thought, because Judas had the bag, that Jesus had said unto him, 'Buy those things that we have need of against the feast,' or that he should give something to the poor."

Judas was the treasurer for the group. It was not unusual for Jesus to send Judas on tasks such as this. Therefore, even though Jesus had announced what He was going to do and by so doing identified Judas as the future traitor, those who were not paying attention missed it. They thought that Judas was just going to do an errand for Jesus. Also in verse 30 we read, "He then having received the sop went immediately out: and it was night."

Indeed, John was the one whom Jesus loved. I believe that John was Jesus' favorite disciple. He obviously had a place close to Jesus, because he was able to physically lean over and place his head on Jesus' chest. Also, Jesus recognized this. Peter asked John to ask Jesus who indeed would betray Him and therefore them. John had a close enough relationship with Jesus that he could ask. He could ask when the others were afraid to. Not only did he ask, but he physically leaned over and placed his head on Jesus' heart.

John received much more by that act of intimacy, that act of seeking Jesus, by touching the Master, than the revelation that Judas would be the betrayer. No, he received much, much more. When he touched Jesus' heart with his head, he learned of the heart of God. And what is the heart of God? Love. It is nothing less than love. It is a love that we cannot understand, as Paul said. It is a love for us so strong that our Father would send Jesus to die for us. "For God so loved the world, that he gave his only begotten Son, that whosoever believeth in him should not perish, but have everlasting life" (John 3:16, KJV). He loves us so much that Jesus willingly came to die for us. He loves us so much that He came to take away our sins so that we who deserve death could live with Him. That is what John learned when he learned what was in the heart of Jesus.

Jesus Himself tells us this. Continuing, we read in John 13:33–35, "Little children, yet a little while I am with you. Ye shall seek me: and as I said unto the Jews, Whither I go, ye cannot come; so now I say to you. A new commandment I give unto you, That ye love one another; as I have loved you, that ye also love one another. By this shall all men know that ye are my disciples, if ye have love one to another."

This command was given to all of the apostles. Only John understood it, however. And John understood it because he had placed his head on Jesus' heart. By doing so, he had learned of Jesus' love. He and only he had done this, so he and only he could understand. We know that the others did not, because immediately Peter ignored this new commandment concerning love and instead concentrated on where Jesus was going. This is given to us in John 13:36–38. These verses read, "Simon Peter said unto him, 'Lord, whither goest thou?' Jesus answered him, 'Whither I go, thou canst not follow me now; but thou shalt follow me afterwards.' Peter said unto him, 'Lord, why cannot I follow thee now? I will lay down my life for thy sake.' Jesus answered him, 'Wilt thou lay down thy life for my sake? Verily, verily, I say unto thee, The cock shall not crow, till thou hast denied me thrice.'"

Therefore, all of them but one missed the command that Jesus had given them. It passed over their heads. They were not able to think on any eternal things. They were not able to think of any Kingdom things. They were wondering who the betrayer was and what they would do. Only John knew. Only John understood, and he understood because he had placed his head on the heart of God. There he found one thing, and that one thing was an unfathomable love that God has for each and every one of us.

When we have God's heart, we have His love. We understand His love. We know His love. We can then reveal and share His love with others.

Jesus has commanded us to feed His flock or sheep. As great as our individual encounter with God is, as great as our Mount of Transfiguration experience may be, we must come down and feed the flock. We can only feed or take care of God's children when we understand and have God's love.

I have asked to see and hear as Jesus did. As I asked for this one day, the Lord answered me and said, "You will as soon as you hear and see as I did. I did not see with my eyes or hear with my ears. Instead, I heard and saw with my heart."

Jesus' mission statement could be summed up as saying that He came to do good works to glorify the Father with compassion in love. If we could ever see and hear as Jesus did, if we can hear and see with our heart instead of with our eyes and ears, then we will understand His love. Then and only then can we truly feed His sheep.

We read in Acts 2:3 of the baptism of fire. This is given to us in Luke 3:16 as well. John the Baptist said that he baptized with water, but that Jesus, one mightier than him, would come and "…baptize you with the Holy Ghost and with fire." What brings about God's fire, which is God's power? It is the baptism of love for the baptism of love is the baptism of fire. If we walk in God's love, if we have God's love, then we can have His power. If we do not walk in love, God cannot give us His power, because we will use His power incorrectly. Jesus Himself said this. In Luke, chapter 9, we read that the people did not receive Jesus (Luke 9:53, KJV). Continuing in verse 54 we read, "And when his disciples James and John saw this, they said, 'Lord, wilt thou that we command fire to come down from heaven, and consume them, even as Elias did?'" What was Jesus' response? In verses 55–56 we read, "But he turned, and rebuked them, and said, 'Ye know not what matter of spirit ye are of. For the Son of man is not come to destroy men's lives, but to save them.' And they went to another village."

Notice that John, along with James, is the one who had asked Jesus this. They had scriptural precedent for this. Elijah did call fire down from Heaven when he defeated and destroyed the false prophets of Baal of King Ahab and Queen Jezebel. Therefore, they assumed that it was proper and expedient for Jesus to do that now. However, Jesus came to give us, with His life, the new covenant. The disciples did not understand this yet. John Himself did not. At this point in their development and walk with God, they were not capable of handling the power of God. If they had the power of God, then they would have used it incorrectly and called down the fire to destroy these people. That was not our Lord's intent and is not His intent now. Rather, His intent is to woo us with love. Therefore, Jesus told and rebuked them that because of their mindset, they were not capable of having God's power.

This was before the Last Supper. This was before John learned of God's love. After he did, then he had the correct spirit, and then God could allow him to use His power as was needed. So too, will God trust us with His power if we walk in and know His love, and obey His commandment to love Him and others as He Himself loves us. Then and only then will we be able to be used by God. Then and only then will God trust us with His power.

God must trust us with His presence before He can trust us with His power. We ourselves are no different. When our sixteen-year-old gets his driver's license, we do not give him the keys to our best car and tell him to go drive unsupervised. No, we have them drive under supervision first or use an old car to see how they do. When they have been found to be trustworthy, then we give them the keys to our own personal or best car. God is no different. If we want to operate with the fire and power of God there is only one way, and that way is through the love of God. John did not know that when he asked Jesus if he would bring fire to come down from Heaven to destroy the people. After he laid his head on Jesus' heart, he did.

To hear from God at any time, we must be at peace. When we are troubled, we cannot hear from God. All the disciples were troubled when Jesus stated at the Last Supper that one of the members of this close group would betray Him. The others could not grasp what Jesus told them. But, there was one who did. That one was John. John could understand Jesus because he was at peace. He was at peace because of his rest and security in Jesus. John was at rest, and because he was at rest with Jesus, he was at total peace. Since he was at peace, he just laid his head on Jesus' chest, and that is where he learned of Jesus and Jesus' love.

We have to be at peace for the Holy Spirit to work in us. The Holy Spirit cannot work or help us in any way if we are not at peace. That is why the enemy tries to do the same thing with us today that he accomplished with the other eleven disciples at the Last Supper. He tries to ignite us to a state of panic, anger, rage or discontent. Anytime he can get us into any kind of emotion, we are not at rest. When we are not at rest with Jesus, then the Holy Spirit cannot use us.

Knowing God's love gives us perfect grace and peace. If we understand God's love there will never be any jealousy or covetousness. When we understand God's love and walk in it, then we will cover one another's faults with love as Peter, who learned this lesson later, did (I Pet. 4:8, KJV). God's love gives us perfect grace and peace. It enables us to remain calm in the middle of the storm when the enemy is attacking us. God's love allows us to be in God's rest with quietness and silence. Love quickens and enables us to walk in the Spirit always. When we do this, nothing will move us.

When Jesus was crucified, all the disciples fled in fear. However, it is heartwarming to know that one of the eleven did seek Him before He rose in triumph from the tomb. One sought Him while He hung on the cross of shame. Who might this one be? Which of the little band of apostles would demonstrate the superiority of Christ's love? It was none other than John. John was found to be at the foot of the cross. There was no hint that the other ten were around the cross, but the one whom Jesus loved was there. John had returned to the Savior's side. There he received the blessed commission to take care of Jesus' mother. John knew Jesus' love more than anyone else. Indeed, he was called the disciple whom Jesus loved.

To know God is to know His love. We will find His love when we seek Him. We will find His love when we seek diligently to have His heart. When we have His love, then, and only then, will God trust us with more of Himself, enabling us to feed His sheep. Let us all aspire to be as John. Let us all aspire to lay our head on Jesus' heart. Let us all aspire to know God and His love the way that John did!

chapter ten

STEP SEVEN:
TO KNOW GOD AS PAUL

And unto the married I command,
yet not I, but the Lord,
Let not the wife depart from her husband.

—I COR. 7:10, KJV

s great as each one of these six separate previous steps are, there is one more step in our journey to be whole, in our journey to be like God, for Jesus commanded us to be like Him. What is that final step? It is to know God, to truly know Him. One may ask if this is possible. It is, because Paul did.

To know God means to have the revelation knowledge of God. This is not head knowledge; rather this is God-speak. It is God's breath breathed into us. It is when the logos or written word becomes alive as the *rhema* word.

What is a revelation? In the natural world we learn through our five senses. We see, hear, taste, smell or touch something. We then assimilate that in our brain. That is knowledge. If we process that knowledge, we then understand it. If we apply what we understand, then that is wisdom. The Bible states that all knowledge, wisdom and understanding comes from God. In II Chronicles 1:1–12, we read where Solomon asked God for wisdom and knowledge, and God granted it to him. Proverbs 2:6 reads, "For the Lord giveth wisdom: out of his mouth cometh knowledge and understanding."

The example that I use is that you may teach your two-year-old to say that two plus two equals four. Although he can repeat it on command, he has no understanding of what this means. Eventually, as he ages, he will understand, and then if he applies it, it will be wisdom.

A revelation from God does not come to us in the same way we acquire natural wisdom. A revelation is spiritual knowledge that bypasses the senses. It is God-speak. It is Spirit unto spirit. It is where God breathes into our spirit man, into our heart. It does not come to us through the natural means. It comes to us only as God-speak to our spirit man. Once we receive that, we must process it. We must assimilate it for it to be useful, not only to us, but to share with others. God speaks it and reveals Himself to us into our spirit man. We then take it to our mind, store it as knowledge, assimilate it as understanding, and then apply it as wisdom. This is spiritual wisdom. The application of spiritual knowledge and understanding is the highest form of wisdom.

The Bible tells us what a revelation is in Matthew, chapter 16. Here we read in verses 13–14 that Jesus asked His disciples who did people say that He was. Then in verse 15, Jesus asked them a very poignant question. He asked them, "…But whom say ye that I am?" He will ask us this question as well. He will ask us this question repeatedly. Jesus is whatever that we think that He is. If we believe that He is our salvation, we will be saved. If we believe that He is our Healer, we will be healed. If we believe that He is able to supply our means, we will prosper. We must be ready, for He will ask us who we believe that He is.

Continuing in Matthew 16:16–17 we read, "And Simon Peter answered and said, 'Thou art the Christ, the Son of the living God.' And Jesus answered and said unto him, 'Blessed art thou, Simon Barjona: for flesh and blood hath not revealed it unto thee, but my Father which is in heaven.'" Here then is the definition of what a revelation is. Peter was the only disciple who was able to answer Jesus' question correctly. Peter, the only one, knew at this particular time that Jesus was the Messiah, the Christ, and the Son of the living God. None of the others did. This is because none of the others had received a spiritual revelation. None of the others had received this revelation from God. Only Peter had. Jesus told them that Peter did not assimilate this through natural means. He did not assimilate this through flesh and blood. No, but it was revealed to him by his Heavenly Father.

This then is what a revelation is. Revelations are the rocks upon which Jesus will build His church. Revelations are the rocks which the gates of hell shall not prevail against (Matt. 16:18, kjv). The revealed word of God, the rhema word, the living word of God, that word which is alive in us because it is God-speak spoken directly to us, is what will give to us the keys to the Kingdom of Heaven. It is what will defeat satan and his minions. It is what will bind on earth what is bound in Heaven, and loose on earth what is loosed in Heaven (Matt. 16:19, KJV).

Paul received more revelation than any man. He wrote most of the New Testament. This was God-speak spoken through him. This was the inspired word of God.

After his conversion, Paul spent three years in the desert, the same desert in the same place that Moses did. Again, to progress on we must complete each of the previous steps. Therefore, Paul had completed most of the steps. After these three years, Paul was then taken to the presence of God in the third Heaven. This is given to us in II Corinthians 12:2, which reads, "I knew a man in Christ about 14 years ago, (whether in body, I cannot tell; or whether out of the body I cannot tell: God knoweth;) such as one caught up to the third heaven." What did he learn there? He learned of God. He knew God. He learned so much that he could write what he wrote in the Bible for us. He learned truths that no man had learned before. He wrote those truths for us. He learned of mysteries which no man knew before. He wrote those mysteries for us. He wrote them so that we could come to know God as he did.

There is more than that, however. II Corinthians 12:4 reads, "How that he was caught up into paradise, and heard unspeakable words, which is not lawful for a man to utter." He learned much more than what he wrote. Some of it was just for him. The same is true for us. When we come to know God, truly know God, when we come to have the scope of revelatory knowledge like Paul had, when we come into the presence of God, when we come to the Holy Throne itself, when we behold the beauty of the Lord and inquire in His temple as David aspired to and sought after but Paul achieved, then God will share things with us that are for us only. There are things that may apply to many others in the world, but they are for us to share with Him in intimacy only. There will be things that the Lord will tell us that we cannot share with others, just like God did with Paul.

I do not believe I know anybody who was as close to God in their walk as Moses was. For sure, I know no one who has accomplished for the Kingdom what Moses did. I am sure that most, if not all of us, if we were to become like Moses, would be happy, content, satisfied, and feel that we had accomplished much. However, as great as Moses was, this was not all that God had for him. It is not all that God has for us. Let us look at some of the differences between Moses and Paul, for Paul pressed on to the mark of the high calling as he spoke, "I press toward the mark for the prize of the high calling of God in Christ Jesus" (Phil. 3:14, KJV).

Moses did not reach his Promised Land. He was not allowed to enter the Promised Land with the rest of the Israelites that he had lead in the wilderness for forty years. Moses continued to petition God to allow him to do so. He asked God three times for God to change his mind and allow him to enter the Promised Land. Finally, God told him to stop asking. God told him specifically to never pray that prayer again. What God did allow him to do was to go to the top of the mountain and get a glimpse of the Promised Land, but he was not allowed to enter the Promised Land.

As you recall, Moses asked God to show him His glory. God told him that He could not do it, because no man could see God and live. Therefore, Moses did not receive this request. God did finally answer Moses' prayer though. He did reveal His glory to him, but it was about 1,500 years after Moses had died. It was on the Mount of Transfiguration when Jesus appeared in His glory and Moses and Elijah were with Him. It was on the same mountain where God had given him the Ten Commandments that God carved with his own finger into the stone. But, God waited 1,500 hundred years to show Moses His glory.

Moses knew where God had been, but he did not know where God was going. He had not seen the glory of God. When God told Moses that as a result of the Israelites stiff-necked ways and rebellion He was no longer going to be with them, Moses beseeched Him to lead them. God said that He would no longer lead them on their journey, but He would send angels to lead them. Moses cried in desperation, and he asked God to change His mind. He said I will not go unless You go before me. "And he said unto him, 'If thy presence go not with me, carry us not up hence'" (Exod. 33:15, KJV).

Certainly, this is a powerful prayer. It has been stated that it is one we should emulate. Powerful? Yes. Poignant? Yes. Necessary? Yes. But one to emulate? Not always. Yes, it is a wonderful prayer. But, if you know God, you not only know where He has been, but where He is going. Moses did not know this. Moses had to ask God to go before Him and lead the way, because He did not know where God was.

Paul never had to pray this prayer once. He knew where God was. He not only knew where God had been, but he knew where God was and where He was going.

The secret for Paul was to totally embrace the cross and allow it to complete its work in him. As John Bevere states:

> The Cross represents complete death to our desires and wishes. Those who embrace the cross trust that God is a faithful, just, and loving Creator and Master. They know that all life comes from Him, and outside Him there is no true life. Moses saw the big picture. Moses understood that God is holy and to draw near to Him required the complete forsaking of the world and its very form. He realized that in denying himself, he would gain the knowledge of God. Paul saw the big picture as well. He was not deceived. He had no desire for the world. The prize for forsaking its pleasures and benefits was no prize at all compared to the unsurpassing greatness of knowing and walking with the One who is life. (*A Heart Ablaze*)

There are so many examples of where Paul wrote this to us. He shared his experience from his heart so that we could come to have the same experience that he did. The following are just a few: "But God forbid that I should glory, save in the cross of our Lord Jesus Christ, by whom the world is crucified unto me, and I unto the world" (Gal. 6:14, KJV); "But what things were gain to me, those I counted loss for Christ. Yea doubtless, and I count all things but loss for the excellency of the knowledge of the Christ Jesus my Lord: for whom I have suffered the loss of all things, and do count them but dung, that I may win Christ" (Phil. 3:7–8, KJV); and "That I may know him, and the power of his resurrection, and the fellowship of his sufferings, being made conformable unto his death" (Phil. 3:10, KJV).

However, Paul understood that this was not a one-time event. Rather, it was something that had to be done constantly. It had to be done daily. Surrendering to God is never a one-time event. As Rick Warren wrote, "There is a moment of surrender, and there is a practice of surrender, which is moment-by-moment and life long." (*The Purpose Driven Life*) Thus Paul could write in I Corinthians 15:31, "…I die daily."

I believe that among the two most important verses for any believer, especially those who are serious about God and their walk with Him, are Matthew 16:24 and Galatians 2:20. Matthew 16:24 reads, "Then said Jesus unto his disciples, 'If any man will come after me, let him deny himself, and take up his cross, and follow me.'" Paul understood this. He knew God. In Galatians 2:20 he wrote, "I am crucified with Christ: nevertheless I live; not yet I, but Christ liveth in me: and the life which I now live in the flesh I live by the faith of the Son of God, who loved me, and gave for himself." He lived, yet he did not, because Christ lived in and through him. He had given his life totally to the Lord.

He had become whole. He lived in the flesh yes, but he lived for Christ and Christ lived through him. And when he lived in the natural world, while he lived in the flesh, it was only by the faith of Jesus.

Paul wanted us to know how to be like him. He wanted us to know how to become whole like he had. He wanted us to know God as he had. Paul knew that it was through the power of the Holy Spirit that the man of God becomes whole. He told us this in II Timothy 3:16–17. These verses read, "All scripture is given by inspiration of God, and is profitable for doctrine, for reproof, for correction, for instruction in righteousness: That the man of God may be perfect, thoroughly furnished unto all good works." We must yield our hearts and lives to the Word for its teaching, reproof, correction and instruction to search and form our entire lives. In this way we will come under the direct operation of God, into full communion with Him, so that us, a man of God, will be whole and "...equipped for every good work."

Paul knew that there was only one way to be whole. That was to embrace the cross and to put his flesh to death daily. It was to walk in the Spirit, which he exhorted us to do so many times. This is the only way. The only way is to be totally dependant upon the Holy Spirit for every aspect of our lives. He realized that this was the only thing that would give him true joy no matter what the circumstances were. Paul himself said that he had learned to be content no matter where he was, what he was doing, or regardless of the circumstances that he found himself in. This included when he was in prison, beaten, stoned to death and shipwrecked.

Regardless of his sufferings, regardless of the conditions he was in, he was content and happy because he had received the joy of the Lord. He had received the joy of the Lord because he had come to rest in the Lord. He had come to rest in the Lord because he had given up all things except the knowledge of Him. He walked with, and was totally dependant upon, God at all times.

Paul was a truly spiritual man. He was led by the Spirit in all that he did. It is God's desire for all of us to become spiritual men as well.

When Adam was created, he was a spiritual man. His spirit was one with God. His spirit controlled all that he did. His soul, which is our mind, will and emotions, was one and in unity with his spirit man. Therefore, his soul and spirit man controlled his flesh. They were in perfect harmony. After the fall, Adam became a fleshly man. We have inherited this from him. We, too, are fleshly men. Adam's soul was no longer in unity or concert with his spirit man. Rather, it was at enmity with the spirit. In fact, until we are converted, we do not have the spirit of God. At our conversion, we receive a new spirit. After our conversion, we must become a spiritual man. We must realign ourselves so that our soul is united with our spirit and our flesh exists to do the work of our spirit man. This is what Paul meant when he wrote that we must work out our salvation. We cannot receive our salvation by works. But once we have received our salvation, we must work out this process of having Christ in us. This is the theme of the book of Colossians. At our salvation we become seated with Christ. We are in Christ. This is the premise of the book of Ephesians. We must then become Christ-like. We do this by dying to ourselves daily. Paul knew this. Paul was whole. Paul was a spiritual man. That is why he said that he had a perfect conscious.

Paul had progressed to the point where he was whole. He had progressed to the point where he was perfect in the eyes of God. Paul had progressed to levels that others had not. I know this because he was able to speak not just the words of God, but for God.

Let us look at I Corinthians, chapter 7. In this chapter, Paul discusses important principles concerning marriage. At first, one would not think that this chapter would be germane to our discussion of Paul being whole, yet it contains the very proof that he was.

If I were to ask you if the Bible is infallible, you would say yes. If I would ask you if it is the Word of God, you would say yes. If I were to ask you if it was written by the Holy Spirit, you would say yes. It was, in fact, written by forty men, but it was written by the Holy Spirit with the words that the Holy Spirit gave the men to write. They were inspired words. They were beyond revealed words. There is, however, an exception to this.

I Corinthians, chapter 7 was not written by the Holy Spirit. Instead, it was written by Paul himself.

Five times in this chapter, Paul states that what he has written in this chapter is not from God, but rather from himself. First, in verse 6 we read, "But I speak this by permission, and not of commandment." Second, in verse 12 we read, "But to the rest speak I, not the Lord. If any brother hath a wife that believeth not, and she be pleased to dwell with him, let him not put her away." Third, in verse 25 we read, "Now concerning virgins I have no commandment of the Lord: yet I give my judgment, as one that hath obtained mercy of the Lord to be faithful." Fourth verse, 10 reads, "And unto the married I command, yet not I, but the Lord, Let not the wife depart from her husband." And fifth, verse 40 reads, "But she is happier if she abide, after my judgment: and I think also that I have the Spirit of God."

Verse 12 summarizes this. Paul clearly states that he was speaking here and not the Lord. This verse reads again, "But to the rest speak I, not the Lord . . ." Paul clearly said that he was speaking and not the Lord. The Lord was not speaking through him here; Paul himself was speaking.

One needs to just stop and reflect on the magnitude of this. The Holy Scripture, with the exception of this chapter, is the direct inspired Word of God. This chapter is also the inspired Word of God as the Bible states that all scripture is. Therefore, what Paul spoke became God-speak.

Paul had gone beyond the revealed Word of God. He had gone beyond being a spokesperson or mouthpiece for the Word of God. He had gone one step further. He was extremely close to God. He knew Him so intimately that he knew what God would speak. In speaking to the Corinthians, he spoke himself. Yet, when he spoke it was if God Himself was speaking. God looked down on what Paul had written and smiled. God said, "Yes, that is what I would have said. But, Paul my servant said it for me. Therefore, what he spoke let it be Mine." God recorded what Paul spoke in this chapter as part of His holy, infallible, inspired Word. Jesus is the Word, and this became part of Him. What Paul spoke, God accepted as His.

Saints, that is how close Paul was to God. Instead of God-speak becoming his speak, what he spoke became God-speak. This is what being complete is. This is what being perfect is. This is what being whole is. Let us indeed aspire to be whole as Paul was.

chapter eleven

CONCLUSION

Till we all come in the unity of the faith,
and of the knowledge of the Son of God,
unto a perfect man, unto the measure of the
stature of the fullness of Christ.

—EPH. 4:13, KJV

Herein we have examined the seven steps to being whole. To be whole means that you have achieved what God wants you to achieve. It means that you have come to rest in Him. It means that you lack nothing. It means that you have joy, even in the face of adversity. It does not mean that you will escape having trials and tribulations. No, we will have these. Satan, our adversary, will do his best to stop and destroy us. He will continue to tempt us. But, we will be victorious because we are whole. We are resting in God. We are perfect in the Lord's eyes and, "No weapon that is formed against thee shall prosper; and every tongue that shall rise against thee in judgment thou shalt condemn. This is the heritage of the servants of the LORD, and the righteousness is of me, saith the LORD" (Isa. 54:17, KJV).

Before we can begin our adventure to becoming whole, we

must first be saved. We must all be born again. We must all be redeemed by the precious Blood of the Lamb, Jesus.

After that, we are assured of eternal life. However, in order to enjoy the promises of God, in order to enjoy our Promised Land, in order for us to walk in victory now, and in order for us to obtain rewards, both in the millennial rule with Christ and eternity, we must press on. We cannot be content to stop with our salvation. Sadly, many do. Most Christians are worldly, carnal or "milk-drinking Christians" as Paul called them. Unfortunately, they have no joy and victory.

No, we must press on! We must go on to become whole. We must do what God wants us to do. We must accomplish what He wants us to do and be what He wants us to be. In order to do that, we must become whole.

The seven steps to becoming whole are: (1) to walk with God as Enoch; (2) to be a friend of God as Abraham; (3) to become a prayer as Joseph; (4) to become a man of God as Moses; (5) to have the heart of God as David; (6) to know God and His love as John; and finally (7) to know God, to truly know God, and to receive His revelatory knowledge as Paul. These are the seven steps to what God wants each of us to accomplish.

Each one of these steps is significant. I am sure if each one of us would obtain even the first step, which is to walk with God, we could, and may well be, totally content. Very few do. Even God would understand. He would continue to use us where we were at that level, for the gifts and callings of God are irrevocable. But, that is not what He wants for each of us. He wants us to move on to the next step. He wants us to pursue Him passionately. He wants us to be all that He has called us to be. He wants us to move past His hand and blessings to know and to be like Him.

The cost is great. That is why so many do not progress. It includes dying to ourselves. It includes embracing the cross and allowing the cross to work its fullness in us. That in itself is painful, but one definition of death is the absence of pain. Jesus will ask us to do nothing that He has not done Himself. What He endured on the cross for us is more than what we have to do for ourselves. He did not just stop at the cross though. No, the cross led Him to the resurrected life. It allowed Him to rise to glory and sit at the right side of the Father once again. It allowed Him to receive His power and majesty. So too, will it be with us if we will but allow God to do what He wants to do with us. If we allow Him to work in us so that we may become Christ-like, we too can pass to the resurrection life. Then, we too, can walk in the power of God. We too, can know God.

It is too hard you might say. It is too difficult. The cost is too much. Yes, this is true, but it is possible and furthermore, it is God's desire. God has never asked us to do anything without giving us the means to do it, nor will He ever. No, He has given us all the means. He has given us His Son and Holy Spirit, and that is all we need. With Him we are more than conquerors, and that includes conquerors over ourselves. If we will but yield our hand to God, He will accomplish in us what He wants. "For it is God which worketh in you both to will and to do his good pleasure" (Phil. 2:13, KJV).

As always, it is we who choose whether this will happen or not. God has given us a will, and He seldom goes against our will. It is His will that we choose to do His will. It is His will that our will match His. We are the ones who alone must choose to walk on this path. "Because straight is the gate, and narrow is the way, which leadeth unto life, and few there be that find it" (Matt. 7:14, KJV). God is here showing the way to all of us. Unfortunately, only a few will choose to follow and find it.

"For many are called, but few are chosen" (Matt. 22:14, KJV). He has called all of us, but few choose to be chosen. There is a cost to be chosen. There is a cost to continue to press on and to be all that God wants us to be. There is a cost to go from each of these levels to the next level. There is a cost to behold. That cost includes not only death to our flesh, but there will be many obstacles, such as family, friends and well-meaning people, including spiritual individuals, who have chosen not to press on. Many will come against and hinder us, and try to keep us from pressing on. I myself have experienced that. I have had well-meaning individuals tell me that I am too spiritual. They have chosen not to pursue God. They have chosen not to understand. It is our choice, and God wants us to press on.

It is possible to become whole. It is possible to become like the men that we have discussed. God used men in the Bible so that we might emulate them. If only Jesus had been whole, we could say it was just because He was Jesus. But, that is not the case. The great patriarchs and men of faith in the Bible were men just like we are. They faced the same battle, physical infirmities, and problems that we do. Yet, they chose to press on. James told us this when he used Elijah as an example. The Bible states that Elijah was a man of God like Moses was. Elijah prayed and altered the course of nature. He prayed that it would not rain, and it did not. He then prayed that it would rain, and it did. James 5:17 reads, "Elias was a man subject to like passions as we are, and he prayed earnestly that it might not rain: and it rained not on the earth by the space of three years and six months."

In Matthew 15:30 we read, "And great multitudes came unto him, having with them those that were lame, blind, dumb, maimed and many others, and cast them down at Jesus' feet; and he healed them." Nothing in the Word is by accident. Why were these people placed in this order? Why were the lame first and then the blind? This parallels the seven steps to becoming whole. The lame must be healed first so that they can walk with God. When we walk with God, then He opens our eyes so that we can see. When we see with His eyes, we have His heart and mind, and we know Him. Then we speak (no longer dumb). We speak to reveal the Word that has been given to us. Then we, the maimed, are made whole. We are restored once again to His image.

Man was originally made in God's image and likeness. Satan stole that from us. We may reach the point where we are restored to whole once again. We can be restored in His likeness. We can be no longer naked but clothed in His glory, like Adam was before He fell. Then, we will be no longer maimed, but whole. Then we can feed His sheep so that they may glorify God.

We need to be whole to be restored to the original Adam.

We need to be whole to be restored to God's image and likeness. Adam, before the fall, was naked, but did not know it. He did not know it because he was whole. When he was whole, he was clothed with God's righteousness, holiness, presence, and His very glory. Adam had this relationship with God. He communed with God in the cool of the day. God commanded him to go and name the animals. He did, and then God sanctioned the words that he used. The knowledge, wisdom and understanding came from God. He was one with God, but the words that he spoke, and the names that he gave them, were his own. God acknowledged and recognized them, and did not change them. They became God's words and names for the creatures.

The same was with Paul. Paul became a yielded vessel and broken. He was still an educated man and gifted speaker. Paul, however, gave all his natural talents to the Lord, and the Lord gave them back to him sanctified and approved for the Lord's use. Paul had been molded and shaped by the potter to the degree where there was nothing of Paul left. Then, he was like the original Adam. Paul's words were spoken by himself, but they became God's words. I, for one, aspire to have this intimacy and relationship with the Father.

Paul wrote in Ephesians 4:13 the following: "Till we all come in the unity of the faith, and of the knowledge of the Son of God, unto a perfect man, unto the measure of the stature of the fullness of Christ." This is what he meant by being whole. A perfect man has the measure of the stature of the fullness of Christ. It is achievable by faith only just as Jesus told the woman with the issue of blood that her faith is what made her whole: "But Jesus turned him about, and when he saw her, he said, 'Daughter, be of good comfort; thy faith hath made thee whole.' And the woman was made whole from that hour" (Matt. 9:22, KJV).

It is God's desire that we all be whole. In fact, He will ask each of us this question just as He asked the man that had been paralyzed for 38 years at the pool of Bethesda. In John 5:6 we read, "When Jesus saw him lie, and knew that he had been now a long time in that case, he saith unto him, 'Wilt thou be made whole?'"

Jesus knows everything there is to know about us. Psalms 139:1 reads, "O Lord, thou hast searched me, and know me." Indeed, He has. He knows everything about us. Since He knows everything about us, He knows where we lie, how long we have been there, and what has been coming against us. Yet, He asks us the same question. That question is "…wilt thou be made whole?" To him there is no excuse to lie in a state of impotence. He has shown us the way. He has paid the price. It is His desire that we be whole.

He knows that this is not an instantaneous process. Rather, it is a lifelong process. It is one, however, that can be achieved. It is also one that He commands us to achieve. In Joshua 1:1–2 we read, "Now after the death of Moses the servant of the LORD it came to pass, that the LORD spake unto Joshua the son of Nun, Moses' minister, saying, 'Moses my servant is dead; now therefore arise, and go over this Jordan, thou, and all his people, unto the land which I do give to them, even to the children of Israel.'" God had to remind even Joshua what he must do. He could not be content with where he was. He had to move on to the next step or level. Moses was dead. It was Joshua's turn to get up and get going to cross over the Jordan River and go to the Promised Land that God had given him. God tells each of us the same thing now. We must not be content to be where we are. We should be content only when we have reached our promised land and the fullness of God. We must move on to the next step. As good at being a man of God as Moses was, it is not all that He wants for us. We must move on. We must cross our Jordan River to reach our promised land.

Andrew Murray writes, "Jesus Christ was Himself not perfected in one day. In Him patience had its perfect work. True faith recognizes the need for time, and it rests in God. The weakest point in the character of the Christian is the measure of His nearness to perfection. It is in little things of daily life that perfection is attained and proved." (*God's Power for Today*, 103) How true! We must go step by step by step.

Frances Roberts has written the following as told to him by God:

Only through suffering can you be made whole, and the purest joys and the reflection of the Holy Spirit's work within the soul. I would not have you anticipate continual elation as the norm of a life of faith. I will manifest Myself to you in times of defeat as well as in the hour of exhilaration. Never have I commanded you to pursue happiness as an end in itself. My Spirit moves within you to reproduce the character of the Lord Jesus Christ so that your whole personality shall ultimately portray the likeness of the new man. This process is often painful because it entails the annihilation of your own person or your own choices. This was the reason the Lord Jesus Christ sweat as is were drops of blood in the hour of His agony in the Garden of Gethsemane. The imagination of the natural mind can not fathom the extent of the inner soul struggle through which a man must pass as he undergoes the transforming process of yielding up the natural will to accept the will of the Spirit...The suffering and passion of the Lord Jesus is in truth a revelation in depth of the very same death struggle of which every soul must pass if God's will is chosen in preference to that of the old carnal mind. "Wherefore let them that suffer according to the will of God commit the keeping of their souls to him in well doing, as unto a faithful Creator." (I Pet. 4:19, KJV)

Glory to God indeed! I hope these words have inspired you as they have me. My prayer for you and me is that we reach our Promised Land and yield to the hand of God, so that we may become whole as well!

finished reading
9-20-12
8:37 PM.
Big Cabin, OK

ABOUT THE AUTHOR

Craig M. Morgan, now fifty-one, is the son of Dr. and Mrs. Willard Morgan. He grew up in Cape Girardeau, Missouri, and attended Grace United Methodist Church. In high school he played football, baseball, and basketball. He then attended Southeast Missouri State University where he was a member of the football team. Subsequently, he attended Vanderbilt University Medical School, and following his graduation there completed a residency in Ophthalmology at the University of California in San Francisco. He then completed a fellowship in retinal disorders at the Massachusetts Eye and Ear Infirmary of Harvard University. At the completion of his training, he worked at the University of Michigan in the Department of Ophthalmology. Then the Lord led him to Huntington, West Virginia, where he and his family have resided for the last 20 years. There he practices Ophthalmology as a retinal specialist. This gives him a unique opportunity to witness to and share his faith with his patients and to behold the miracles of healing that the Lord does.

He was married in 1977, and he and his wife, Pam, have one son, Craig, married to their daughter-in-law, Andrea. The Lord has also brought them two families that have become part of their own, Tim and Una Martin and their three children, Rosy, Timmy, and Tony; and B.J. and Tosha Roberts and their four children, Micaiah, Josiah, Nehemia, and Zachariah.

Although saved earlier, his true conversion occurred on February 25, 1998, through a close encounter with the Lord. After that he dedicated every aspect of his life to serving, walking after and knowing the Lord. He and his family attend Christ Temple Church in Huntington, West Virginia, where Chuck Lawrence is the Senior Pastor. Craig himself was ordained as a pastor on December 31, 2003.

Still an avid sportsman, he likes to fish and hunt, pursuing both big game fishing and hunting.

He has authored many scientific articles and publishes a teaching each week that the Lord has given him on his website: www.fromthemouthofgod.com. However, this is his first book. He would ask that you pray for him so that he may come to know our Lord in a new and greater way and be able to convey this to others in a meaningful fashion.

FROM THE MOUTH OF GOD

From the Mouth of God is the ministry of Craig M. Morgan. Craig's desire is to share with you the many teachings that our Lord has shown him through his in-depth study of the Word and every day close walk with our Heavenly Father. His prayer is that when you are weary, you will run to the lap of Jesus where your spirit will be renewed and refreshed by His very presence.

Craig's weekly teachings will challenge you to die daily to self and its desires, while simultaneously teaching you how to live this life with courage to continue this journey till the day of His return. You can make it!

JOIN US EVERY WEEK:

Every Friday a new teaching is posted on Craig's Web site: fromthemouthofgod.com

HOW TO CONTACT US:

By Internet: fromthemouthofgod.com
By Mail: From the Mouth of God
1611 13th Avenue
Huntington, WV 25701

Craig would like to thank Karen Salters, who types and prepares the teachings for his website, www.fromthemouthofgod.com. He is very grateful to John Wills for his ingenuity in creating and maintaining his Web site.